# A
# Thames
# Companion

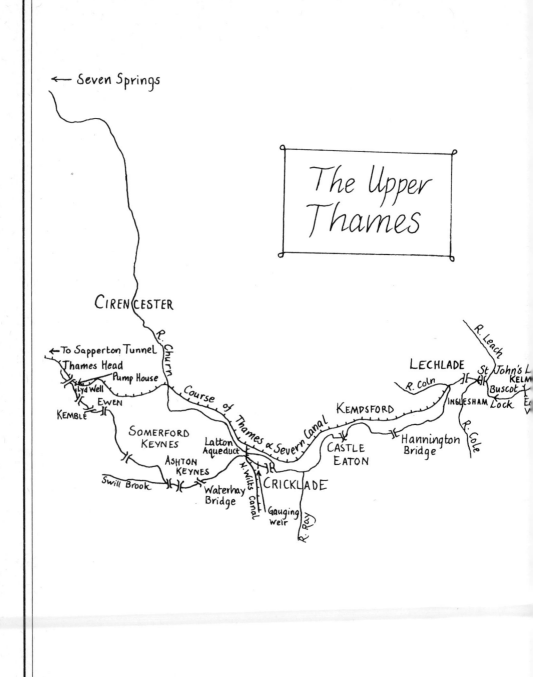

← Seven Springs

The Upper Thames

CIRENCESTER

← To Sapperton Tunnel
Thames Head
Pump House
Lyd Well
Ewen
KEMBLE

R. Churn

Course of Thames & Severn Canal

SOMERFORD KEYNES

ASHTON KEYNES

Swill Brook

Latton Aqueduct

Waterhay Bridge

N. Wilts Canal

Gauging Weir

CRICKLADE

R. Ray

CASTLE EATON

KEMPSFORD

Hannington Bridge

LECHLADE

R. Coln

R. Leach

St John's L
Buscot
Lock
INGLESHAM
KELM
E

R. Cole

scale  0  1  2  3  4  5  6  miles

M.P.

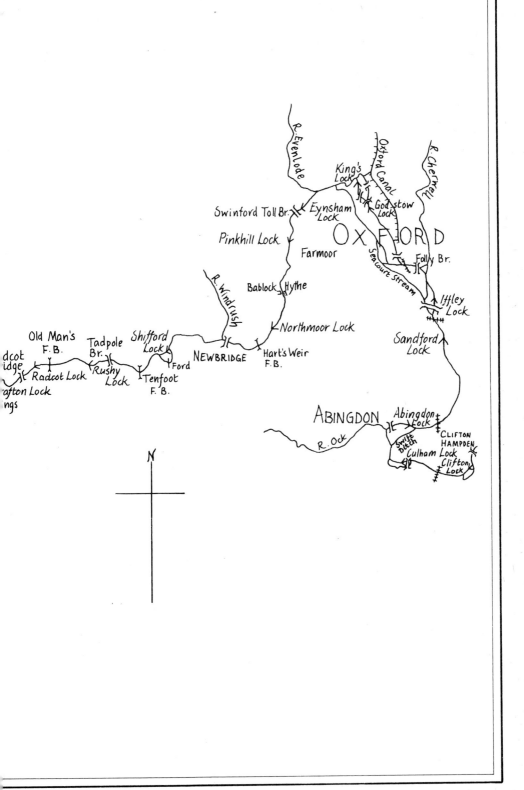

R. Evenlode

Oxford Canal

R. Cherwell

King's Lock

God stow Lock

Swinford Toll Br.

Eynsham Lock

OXFORD

Pinkhill Lock

Farmoor

Seacourt Stream

Folly Br.

R. Windrush

Bablock Hythe

Iffley Lock

Northmoor Lock

Sandford Lock

Shifford Lock

Old Man's F.B.

Tadpole Br.

dcot idge

Radcot Lock

Rushy Lock

Ford

NEWBRIDGE

Hart's Weir F.B.

Tenfoot F.B.

afton Lock ngs

ABINGDON

Abingdon Lock

R. Ock

Swift Ditch

Culham Lock

CLIFTON HAMPDEN

Clifton Lock

N

# A
# Thames
# Companion

Mari Prichard &
Humphrey Carpenter

© Oxford Illustrated Press Ltd, Mari Prichard and
Humphrey Carpenter, 1975

Set in 10/12pt Monotype Baskerville by Bristol & West Engravers Ltd

Printed and bound in Great Britain by Ebenezer Baylis & Son, Worcester

Oxford Illustrated Press Ltd, Shelley Close, Headington, Oxford

PHOTOGRAPHS

Except in those cases where we have specified to the contrary, the
contemporary photographs in the book were taken by ourselves. We are
most appreciative of the skill with which Paul Lucas of Thomas Photos
(Oxford) produced such excellent prints from our amateur negatives.

Mari Prichard & Humphrey Carpenter.
Oxford, 1975.'

# Contents

# Introduction and Acknowledgements

'One of the famousest rivers in England'
Anthony à Wood, *City of Oxford*, I.397

This book follows the course of the River Thames from its source to its estuary, in words and in pictures. It recounts the history of the navigation, and records the character of the Thames today and the character of some of the people whose working lives are bound up with it.

It has been compiled after many river trips, in every type of craft from inflatable dinghy to tideway tug (not to mention walking-boots for the towpath). Our thanks are due to all those people whose assistance and courtesy has made the task such a pleasure. The majority of these are mentioned by name in the text, but there are others to whom we wish to record our gratitude.

Particular thanks are owed to Mr R. R. Bolland, who has helped us in numerous ways. From his unrivalled collection of Thames books come the photographic reproductions (made by himself) of eighteenth and nineteenth century plates of the river. He has also supplied several photographs, ancient and modern, and has read our manuscript, correcting a number of errors. Mr J. P. Wells, Oxford City Librarian, has allowed us to reproduce a number of unique photographs by Henry Taunt which are in the library's archives, and Mr Malcolm Graham has given us assistance in selecting them and arranging for reproduction. Other suppliers of illustrations, to whom we owe our thanks, are mentioned by name in the relevant captions to the pictures.

Mr Ron Coates of the *Swindon Evening Advertiser* provided the picture of the Polish water-walker and the information about him. The Vicar of Kempsford gave us kind hospitality and much information about his church and its surroundings. Messrs Chris Rayson, Stan Day, Harry Kimber and E. A. Pocock all helped us with our research into the history of Radcot Bridge. Dr Tom Hassall of the Oxford Archaeological Excavation Committee supplied material about the Trill Mill Stream. Mr Jim Butler and Mr John Salter helped with information about the history of Salter's Steamers, and lent a valuable photograph. Mr F. D. Godsell of the Thames Water Authority took pains to provide detailed answers to our many questions. Mr John

Garton, Chairman of Henley Royal Regatta, gave us much assistance. Mr John McArthur of the Port of London Authority, and P.C. John Joslin of Thames Division, Metropolitan Police, were most helpful in providing material for the final chapter. Mr Andrew Howard of Humphery & Grey (Lighterage) Ltd arranged for us to travel on his firm's tug *Grey Lash*, and subsequently checked and corrected the part of the text concerning that journey. The crew and lightermen on board the tug made our day's trip memorable for their generosity and friendliness.

The book could scarcely have been written without the facilities of the Bodleian Library, and Mr Ron Tandy, of the Bodleian's topographical section, has given us much assistance in tracing rare books and illustrations.

Finally our thanks must go to Robert Campbell, who suggested that we should write the book, to Jane Marshall, who has nursed it through the press, and to our companion on two memorable Thames voyages, Roger Green, who after prolonged exposure to sunburn, uncomfortable camp beds, damp blankets, and leaking boats, still shares our enthusiasm for the river which flows past his door.

# Prologue

'The River Thames' seems to be the plainest, most English of names; but any attempt to establish its origins lands us at once in controversy.

There are seven rivers in England with similar names: the Thame, which flows into the Thames near Dorchester and gives its name to an Oxfordshire town; the Tame which forms the border between Lancashire and Cheshire; another Tame in Yorkshire; the Tam at Tamworth; the Team in County Durham; the Teme which flows from North Wales into the Severn below Tenbury; and the Tamar in the West Country.

But these names are not peculiar to the English language. There are similarities in other continents. For instance, one of the tributaries of the Ganges bears the Sanskrit name *Tamasa*. So what is the root of meaning held in common by all these rivers? Philologists generally agree it to be *teme*, meaning 'dark' (which can be found for instance in the Latin *tenebrae*, 'the shades'). Whether the waters of all these rivers can be called dark is a matter of opinion; certainly the Thames at London is murky, but with contamination that the ancient Britons could scarcely have forseen. Or perhaps these rivers often *seemed* dark, mysterious and fearsome, especially in their lower and more dangerous reaches. Moreover, the Celtic tribes were inclined to river-worship, which may have increased their sense of rivers as dark and mysterious.

The first recorded appearance of the name 'Thames' in any shape or form dates from two thousand years ago, and comes in Julius Caesar's account of his exploits in Britain. To him it was the river *Tamesis*, which is simply a Latinization of what the local inhabitants called it. This form of the name became accepted all over the classical and classically-educated world.

Meanwhile the Barbarians had their turn at influencing the river's name. Some six hundred years after Caesar, the Angles, Saxons and Jutes overran his colony, and the River Thames became, by invasion, English. When the name came to be written down in Alfred's time it was spelt *Temes*. It is not strange that the Anglo-Saxons took the old British name of the river they

The Upper Thames above Shifford.

won; conquerors almost always use river names as they find them, merely
changing the pronunciation a little to suit their own language. What *is*
strange, according to philologists, is the preservation of the letter -s at the
end of *Temes* (and thus at the end of the modern name). In all the other
similar English river names the final -s once almost certainly existed but, at a
time of linguistic change before the names were first recorded, the letter
ceased to be sounded. The argument is that the Anglo-Saxons heard of the
name of the Thames and learnt it *before* that time, probably before they
reached Britain and settled there; knew it perhaps because it was already a
famous river, an estuary of importance for piracy and trade. The very fame
of the river seems to have preserved its name in the old form.

The Old English word *Temes* is not very different from the way the name
is pronounced today; the rather strange spelling *Thames* is of slightly different
origin. It seems to have come about because of the influence of French and
Latin, the 'smart' languages of the Middle Ages. As we have seen *Tamesis*
was the Latin name for the river, and to make the English name seem more
Latin, people began to write it *Tames*; then, to make it more French, *Thames*.
That form first appeared in the sixteenth century: it was printed, and it
stuck.

If you have ever encountered (or have yourself been) a stickler for correct

Punts under Goring Bridge.

Oxford expressions, you will have come across the belief that the Thames at Oxford should properly be called the Isis: hence the Isis boat crew, the name of an undergraduate magazine, and many other Oxford names. According to this tradition, 'Isis' is the true name of the river from its source until it meets the Thame at Dorchester, whereupon the confluence of rivers produces a confluence of names, and we have Thame-Isis or Thamesis; hence Thames. This belief is still quite widely held, but it poses several problems. First, the geographical one: the Thame is a fairly small tributary of the Thames and has no particular importance; it is scarcely likely to make the main river change its name at the confluence. Second, there is no evidence that the name Isis as applied to the upper reaches of the river has any real antiquity; its first recorded use is by Ranulph Higden in 1350 (very late in the river's history) and even he refers to the river at its source as the Thames. Isis was the name of an Egyptian goddess, and seems to have been adopted by the University of Oxford, which wanted to re-christen its river with a name of classical associations. It has been mainly the University that has spent the last six hundred years trying to persuade the rest of us to adopt the name. Are we to be so easily led?

# I

# Stripling Stream: The Source to Cricklade

If you want to be thorough about visiting the source of the Thames, you will
have to make not one journey but two. First of all, go and find Seven Springs.

The most pleasant way is to journey up the Churn Valley from Cirencester
towards Cheltenham. Keep on past the splendid Cotswold place-names of
Baunton, Bagendon, Woodmancote and Rendcomb, until you are nearly in
the village of Coberley. Then, where the A435 crosses the A436, turn left
and look for a lay-by a few yards along the road. Here, a few feet below road
level, half hidden by cars and picnic parties, are the Seven Springs which
some people consider to be the true source of the Thames. Crawl along a
stone ledge above the water and you will even see a tablet claiming this in
Latin:

HIC TUUS
O TAMESINE PATER
SEPTEMGEMINUS FONS

The 'sevenfold fountain' is a few feet below. Not all seven of the springs may
be visible, but you can generally count at least five rivulets bubbling from
the Cotswold stone wall into the basin.

The river that begins its life at Seven Springs is called the Churn. Nobody
argues about that, but there are people who think that the Churn deserves
the title 'Thames' better than the stream which rises at Thames Head, near
Kemble. Certainly there are various scientific facts to support this view.
Thames Head is only 356 feet above sea level, while the Seven Springs are
at an altitude of 700 feet. They are also further from the sea than Thames
Head. And the Seven Springs do not usually dry up. They are recorded as
yielding between 100,000 and 3,780,000 gallons of water a day, according to
the season; whereas the yield of the headspring at Thames Head on many
days of the year is nil.

In February 1937 the rival claims of the two sources were debated in the
House of Commons. Mr Perkins, Member for Stroud, asked the Minister of

Seven Springs.

Agriculture whether he was aware that the latest edition of the Ordnance Survey map marked the source as Thames Head? Would the Minister give an undertaking that in the next edition the words 'Source of the Thames' would be transferred to Seven Springs, in his constituency? The Minister (Mr Morrison) would not; but then he must also be suspected of having a local interest, as *his* constituency was Cirencester and Tewkesbury, and Thames Head is very near Cirencester. The debate continued like this:

> *Mr Perkins:* Is the right hon. Gentleman aware that the source known as Thames Head periodically dries up?
> *An Hon. Member:* Why don't you? (*Laughter*).

Despite Mr Perkins, Thames Head is still accepted as the source by most authorities.

### THAMES HEAD

The 'official' source is not easy to find. From Cirencester, take the main road towards Tetbury. This is the old Foss Way to Bath, and like most Roman roads it runs straight. People drive ferociously along it, overtaking in all the wrong places, so you will have to be careful if you want to reach Thames Head in one piece. A few minutes away you will see that the road has been

Water visible at Thames Head before the removal of the statue.

widened creating a little cul-de-sac on the right. Here is a strange corrugated-iron cottage which seems to have started life as a chapel. Stop here and have a look at your surroundings: you are now standing on what was once a bridge over the Thames & Severn Canal. The stone houses in the hollow were officially called Thames Head Wharf, and this wharf served the district for seven miles around with cargo from the canal. But the navigation (which ran from near Lechlade through to the Bristol Channel) was closed in 1927, the waterway has been bone dry for decades, and nowadays it is difficult to imagine the painted canal boats carrying their cargo to and from London and the Severn ports by way of this bramble-choked ditch.

Go down the road for a hundred yards or so, and turn right into a field. Unless the weather has been very wet you will not see any water; nevertheless you are looking at the very topmost half-mile of the Thames. Walk across the first field and into the second, which is called Trewsbury Mead. In the far right-hand corner, near the canal embankment, is a big ash tree on whose trunk someone many years ago carved the initials 'T.H.' They stand for 'Thames Head'. For you are now at the accredited source of the Thames, in the parish of Coates, in the county of Gloucestershire.

Thames Head as pictured in *History of the Principal Rivers of Great Britain* (1794).

Until April 1974 a Victorian statue of Father Thames stood here. But it was a popular target for vandals, despite the railings that protected it; and eventually the Thames Conservancy removed it, had it restored, and placed it by St John's Lock at Lechlade, the highest lock on the river. Now a plain stone block marks the source.

But where is the water? It *ought* to be in the little hollow at the foot of the ash tree. But for most of the year all that can be seen there is a heap of stones (and somebody's sweet-papers or lemonade tins). If we are to believe tradition, there was once a lively spring here with water visible all the year round. In William Combe's *History of the Principal Rivers of Great Britain*, which was published for John and Josiah Boydell in 1794, the author describes Thames Head as follows:

> The spring rises in a well of about thirty feet in depth, inclosed within a circular wall of stone, raised about eight feet from the surface of the meadow, with a trough of the same materials before it, into which the water is thrown by a pump to supply the cattle of the adjacent villages. In the driest season this spring never fails; and in the winter, it sometimes not only flows over the wall, but issues from the earth around the well, and, forming an ample stream, winds through the meadow.

But this does not appear to have been written from personal experience. Combe continues:

> In the month of June, when we visited the spring, it was sunk considerably beneath its natural margin; and its winter course was discoverable only by a path of rushes, which serpentined along the valley.

So perhaps Combe sent the artist who drew the picture of the well to Thames Head in a wet season; perhaps his drawing of water flowing over the sides of the well is artistic licence; or perhaps one of the bystanders has just worked the pump-handle. Certainly this account gives no confirmation that the spring was substantially more active in 1794 than it is today.

In fact we have an account from the sixteenth century indicating that even in those days the spring was producing no surface water for some of the year. John Leland, the much travelled library-keeper to Henry VIII, wrote in his *Itinerary*: 'Wher as the very head of Isis ys, in a great somer drought apperith very little or no water.'

### THE WATER DIVINER

During February 1974, a great deal of rain fell in the South East of England. The Thames was in flood, and with water levels high it was obviously a good occasion to examine Thames Head. We visited it one day when all the other springs in the area were active, expecting to find that it, too, was bubbling over into the fields. But there was only a pool of stagnant water at the foot of the ash tree, and no signs of an active spring. So was the source of the Thames really 'dead'? It seemed possible. To get an expert view on the matter we decided to engage the services of somebody who has spent much of his time locating underground springs and analysing their strength.

When Mr John Sawyer, a water diviner of Oxford, was asked by us to come to Thames Head and give his opinion on the state of the spring, he was delighted; it was, he said, out of the usual run of his work (which chiefly consists of telling people where to sink wells, and diagnosing underground streams as the cause of basement damp). Mr Sawyer, who was 79 at the time of our visit, prefers to be called a 'dowser', as that name has less of a magical ring than 'water divining'. He believes that dowsing is perfectly scientific, if imperfectly understood: he says that it operates on a kind of geiger-counter principle—and indeed you can dowse for metal just as well as for water. He suggests that both water and metal give off some kind of electrical pulse to which certain people are sensitive (he finds that about one person in fifteen can dowse); and to cynics he simply points out that he has had many years of excellent results. He has been dowsing part-time since 1930. Sinking a well,

5

Mr John Sawyer 'dowsing' at Thames Head.

he says, is an expensive job; the dowser has to be right, or people will not go on employing him. As we have said, the job of tracing underground water at Thames Head appealed to Mr Sawyer, his only conditions being that he should wait until spring and drier weather (surface water would be confusing), and that he should be told as little as possible about where the water was likely to be found.

Mr Sawyer and his wife were driven to Thames Head on 7 April, 1974. The day was fine, no rain had fallen for about a week, and the fields were quite dry. A very little way along the path into Trewsbury Mead Mr Sawyer decided to make the first test, to find out in which direction he should go. He took from the basket which his wife was carrying a pair of whalebone rods, about ten inches long, and joined at one end with sticking plaster. Whalebone, he told us, was just as good as a split hazel twig (the traditional dowser's rod) and did not break so easily.

Mr Sawyer stood with his arms outstretched, the rods in one hand; he shook them, then was still for a moment. After a few seconds he marched off confidently into the middle of the field and then began some more precise dowsing. This time he held the whalebones open, one end in each hand, with the apex pointing downwards to the ground; he was now standing some thirty feet from Thames Head itself. After a few tries he got a response; the rods began to twitch, and then spun right round in his hands with a force of their own. 'That's it,' said Mr Sawyer, 'there's water under there.' He began to follow the course of the underground stream, the rods now turning over regularly in his hands. In a few moments he had reached the spot which he declared to be the source of the stream: the pile of stones by the ash tree that marks Thames Head. 'That's it', said Mr Sawyer, 'that's where the water comes from, under there. Now do you want to find out how deep down the water is?'

This task required a different tool, a rough loop of thin copper wire terminating in a coiled handle. 'Nothing specially made,' said Mr Sawyer, 'just a bit of wire. Now, count the number of times it turns over. Each turn is about two foot.' The wire in Mr Sawyer's hand turned over once, twice, and then very nearly a third time; then it stopped. 'Five feet,' he said. 'If you dig down five or six feet you'll come to water.' How much water, we asked? Mr Sawyer took out the whalebones again and did some more tests; he established the position first of one side of the stream, then the other. The marks were about ten inches apart. 'That means it's ten inches wide,' he told us, 'about the equivalent of a ten-inch diameter pipe. There's plenty of water there if only you dig down to it.'

### LYD WELL

There is water to be *seen* very near to Thames Head, if you are prepared to do a little walking. Leave the ash tree and the pile of stones, and cross the fields back towards the Foss Way. Water runs freely here in wet weather, and there are perhaps half a dozen minor springs between Thames Head and the road. For, as Leland wrote in the sixteenth century, the Thames is 'servid with many springs resorting to one bottom'. But for most of the year you will have to walk further to find the first signs of the river as a flowing stream.

When you get into the field on the other side of the road (that is, south of the Foss Way) you may see the beginnings of a stream in the little valley. One of the more important springs is here; it is hard to find in dry weather, but after heavy rain the water comes bubbling out of the ground, crystal clear and fresh to taste. But let us assume that on the day of your visit the little spring here is dry. Walk along the bed of the infant river (or by it, for the ground is soft and damp even in summer). Note the rudimentary stone bridges (the first footbridges over the Thames); these were very necessary in winter. Pass the old pump-house on your left and cross into the second field. Here you will see two landmarks: Kemble church spire peeping over the trees, and a windpump in the corner of the field. Go down to the windpump (which is now disused) and here you will find Lyd Well.

7

Lyd Well in winter.

Lyd Well means 'loud spring' in Old English, and the name is well earned: after wet weather the water thunders out of the ground. The spring may not be running today if the weather has been particularly dry; if that is the case, step gingerly to the well's margin and look down through the grating; then you will certainly be rewarded by the sight of water. At most times of the year there will be no chance of getting so close: in the winter the water forces itself up through the circular opening in a cascade many inches high, flooding the little hollow at the side of the field. Thousands of gallons a day rise to the surface here and rush past the windpump to join the parent stream on its journey to Kemble, Ewen and Cricklade.

Lyd Well is mentioned in Domesday Book and is thought by some to be Roman. Its origins cannot be established with certainty, but it is near the Foss Way and is set in a landscape dotted with Roman remains. Cirencester was the second most important town in Roman Britain; it was two-thirds the size of London and was the capital of the richest part of Britain, the Cotswolds. Whoever sank the well could not have chosen a better spot; it is said to be the very last site at which water fails in the valley. The water itself is recorded as being fourteen feet deep in the upper beds of the stone known as the Great Oolite.

8

The canal pump-house near Thames Head (1811).

### THE PUMP-HOUSE AND THE WATER LEVEL

On your way across the fields to Lyd Well you pass the old pump-house of the Thames & Severn Canal. It stands on one side of the canal embankment, and until a few years ago it was an eerie place, the ruins standing gaunt, derelict and dangerous because of an open well-shaft. Now it has been rebuilt as a private house. In its time it was the cause of much controversy.

The canal ran from the Thames at Inglesham (near Lechlade) across Gloucestershire to the Severn Estuary. Its summit-level at Thames Head was always short of water, there being few natural supplies. To make matters worse, what water could be found was often lost again through seepage in the very porous soil; in places the canal bed has been lined with concrete to help retain water. Early in the canal's life, the company decided to try and pump water up from the meadows between the Foss Way and Kemble, as they were known to be full of subterranean water supplies ('numerous little Fountains' as a contemporary writer described them). The engineers sank trial bores and installed first a 'wind engine', and then a steam pump. The pump-house was built and the engine, a Boulton & Watt single-acting beam engine, arrived in 1792. It was of 53.2 hp, and was designed to work a pump twenty-six inches in diameter lifting water seventy feet at a rate of ten strokes a minute.

The engine came into service in June 1794. It worked from then on for more than a hundred years with only a rare overhaul, pumping from twelve to twenty-four hours a day depending on how much water was needed. For much of its life it was tended by an engineer called Thomas Toward, who

9

'worked boath early and whoal nights & Sundays when necessity required it'. In 1883 he gave notice, 'after fulfillin a Sarvitude of 42 years as the Local Engineer'. His name was incised upon one of the stones of the old engine-house and survived there until a few years ago.

No sooner did the pump begin to work than it became the target of abuse. The Squire of Kemble threatened to sue the canal company because the pumping (he claimed) had drained the wells in his village. Authorities on the Thames claimed that the pump was drawing water away from the head-springs of the river; in particular it was urged that the pumping was responsible for Thames Head itself being dry for most of the year. Henry Taunt, the Oxford photographer and Thames enthusiast, wrote in the 1880s: 'In olden times, before the construction of the navigation [i.e. the canal] this spring would often be flowing; but owing to the action of the Thames Head Pump, which drains the water out of the springs, it only runs at rare intervals, and these only when the pump is still. The springs of the valley appear to have diminished in volume and force.' Taunt was recording this only from hearsay; he was born in 1842 and was not alive to see Thames Head before the pump had started to work. But his explanation of the apparent drought at Thames Head was commonly held to be true, and is repeated by other Victorian writers.

It was scarcely fair: the pump itself did not draw a vast quantity of water, and was only connected to springs within about five hundred yards of the pump-house (Thames Head is three-quarters of a mile away). Furthermore, the canal company's own engineer John Taunton recorded in 1882 that the general water level in the valley did not seem to be affected permanently by the pumping: 'The water level [in the pump-house well] varies from 30 to 53 ft below the surface, according to the season and pumping. When the engine pumps continuously, it usually lowers the water level gradually, in a dry season 3 or 4 inches a week. There does not appear to be any material change in the normal level of the water.' (Quoted by L. Richardson, *Wells & Springs of Gloucestershire*, 1930).

Now the canal is closed, and the pump has long since been dismantled and removed, and still no water appears at Thames Head in normal weather conditions. The canal and the pump can scarcely have been to blame for what is (as we learnt earlier) a very ancient state of affairs.

Near here, the canal runs for 3,817 yards through the great Sapperton Tunnel, one of the finest feats of eighteenth century engineering. One mouth of the tunnel is within walking distance of Thames Head, close to the village of Tarlton; the Tunnel House Inn stands by it. The other mouth is hidden in the woods above the Daneway Inn at Sapperton. A careful study of the one-inch Ordnance Survey map will lead you to it. The tunnel is only a few feet wider than the boats which passed through it, and traffic was strictly single

Sapperton Tunnel.

file, with a one-way system operating by timetable so that boats should not meet head on. The heavily laden craft were propelled by 'leggers' walking along the sides or the roof of the tunnel; they could be hired at either end, and the inns near the tunnel mouths provided them with refreshment. The tunnel is now blocked in at least one place by falls of rock, and is dangerous to explore.

### THE FIRST MILLS

From Lyd Well to Kemble (a little over a mile to the south of Thames Head) the river is scarcely more than a trickle for most of the year. It meanders through meadows, its surface sometimes dotted with the white flowers of water crowfoot. It collects other rivulets, but is still shallow and unnavigable as it runs through the little tunnel under the road near Kemble, and comes out into the fields above Ewen.

'Ewen' means 'source of a river' in Old English, and though the village is some distance from Thames Head we are still in source-land. You would

Ewen Mill, from Mr & Mrs Hall's *Book of the Thames* (1859).

scarcely think there was enough water to turn a mill-wheel, yet here stood
the highest water-mill on the Thames. Ewen Mill was alongside the road
from Kemble, near Parker's Bridge; it was active for many centuries. Mr and
Mrs S. C. Hall, a Victorian couple who wrote *The Book of the Thames*, visited
it in the 1850s: 'The mill [they wrote] is sufficiently rude in character to be
picturesque: it is an open court, fronted by an old pigeon-house, and
occupied by a pleasant and kindly miller, who reasonably complains that
the engine of the canal [i.e. the pump near Thames Head] frequently leaves

him without water to move his wheel.' Today the place is still called Mill Farm, but now there is no sign of mill machinery. A huge grain silo dominates the cluster of farm buildings; it is impossible to tell where among them the mill-wheel would have been sited. Likewise the exact course of the mill-stream, now mostly filled in, can only be guessed at.

Until the present century, mills were an important feature of all rivers, not least the Thames. They provided flour and other grain products for the neighbourhood, and sometimes motive power for paper-making and other purposes. The miller was an influential figure, his influence extending to the river itself. A mill-stream was used (or dug) to supply the mill-wheel, while a by-pass stream carried the rest of the water, the flow being controlled by a sluice. If the river was low, the miller would divert most of the water to the mill-wheel. In the navigable part of the river this was obviously to the detriment of the boatmen who had to navigate the by-pass stream, and craft could become stranded, with resulting disputes between the barge crews and the miller or his men, sometimes leading to violence. Even when water was not short, a miller would only let a barge pass his weir when it suited him, and could (and usually did) also demand a heavy toll.

Mills, then, were one reason for digging a new channel. There were several others: for instance, to improve the navigation, or to provide a deeper watercourse where the river was likely to flood. This has been done on one stretch of the Thames between Ewen and Somerford Keynes, where many years ago a new cut was dug to improve the flow; it runs a straight course alongside the meandering stream (now nearly dry) which was the original path of the river.

More mills stood near here, but now only their names remain: Upper Mill Farm, Old Mill Farm. The next with something to show is Kemble Mill between Poole Keynes and Somerford Keynes. This, like all the others, is in private hands and is not normally open to the public. But it does contain interesting relics of machinery, including two pairs of millstones still in position on an upper floor. The water-wheel remained until recently, but was eventually removed because debris caught against it and blocked the stream. (Mill-wheels can be troublesome: if they are left in position and allowed to turn freely they make a terrible amount of noise and are often taken away for that reason.) Kemble Mill has not worked since the early years of this century; but Lower Mill at Somerford Keynes was in use until only a few years ago, and is still in working order. In its last years of operation it used to grind cattle-feed for use on the adjacent farm.

In Britain today only a handful of water-mills remain in use for their original purposes. A few of these are to be found in Gloucestershire near the Thames, though none is situated on that river. Since the fuel crisis of 1973 the question of the economic generation of power has been in many

Sluice at Lower Mill, Somerford Keynes.

people's minds, and it has been suggested that small water-mills might contribute to national resources by driving electric generators to supply local communities. Meanwhile the Thames water-mills stand idle, and the river's power runs to waste.

### WATERHAY BRIDGE: THE HIGHEST BOAT TRAFFIC

The river takes several paths through the village of Ashton Keynes, and collects the substantial Swill Brook on the way. Now considerably increased in volume, it flows beneath Waterhay Bridge.

The present bridge is a modern structure of steel and concrete. The spot is rather bleak, and seems insignificant until you read what Taunt has to say about it: 'In all probability the Thames was once navigable to this point for boats of 7 tons burden, which conveyed cheese, corn, etc., the produce of the county, to the storehouses still in existence below Lechlade, where they were reloaded into larger boats and sent down to London and other towns down the river. This theory seems to be confirmed by the existing vestiges of several weirs at and above Cricklade.' This belief is repeated by Thacker, but neither writer gives any source for the information, and we can find no local tradition to support it.

14

Footbridge near Upper Waterhay.

To navigate above Cricklade, it is better to use a canoe or some other very light craft; and if you are law-abiding you should ask the permission of the landowners along the banks, for the right of navigation does not extend above Cricklade, and technically this is private water. There are also physical barriers in the shape of barbed wire fences at a foot or less above water level, erected across the river to prevent cattle straying. If they are efficiently staked to the river bed, and choked with fallen branches, they can be impenetrable.

But if you are still determined to make the trip, and are prepared to squeeze under the wire or scramble up the bank and around it, then it is possible to start at High Bridge, Ashton Keynes, where there is a convenient landing-point, and make a slow progress downstream. You will need to be suitably dressed for walking on the stony bed of the river, dragging the boat when the water is shallow; and for carrying it round obstacles. To this latter operation canoeists give the grand title of 'portaging', which is small consolation for the sweat of doing it.

There are few landmarks between Waterhay Bridge and Cricklade: two or three farms, several tributary brooks joining the river, and the occasional footbridge; these are the only features by which you can mark your slow progress. But no two footbridges are the same. Near Brook Farm, Upper Waterhay, the river is spanned by a terrifying structure, made of rough stone supporting massive but grey and worm-eaten beams. Already, essential parts of this footbridge seem to have slipped into the water; old corrugated iron holds another section in place. You pass underneath as quickly as you can, certain that a mere whisper, much more the touch of an oar or a paddle, will bring the bridge's centuries of existence to a sudden and dusty end.

There are other bridges, more secure and formal. They may only serve the needs of a farm, but their builders took trouble, and they generally boast at least one perfect arch. They can be seen as miniatures, models of the greater and more famous bridges further down the river.

Shortly before the river reaches Cricklade it passes the site of the former Latton aqueduct, which carried the North Wiltshire Canal from its junction with the Thames & Severn Canal, a few hundred yards away, to meet the Wilts & Berks Canal at Swindon. The aqueduct was opened in 1819 and was built of solid masonry, the Thames running beneath it through culverts. Now the aqueduct, like the canal it carried, has vanished. Instead, a simple wooden footbridge spans the river. So it is possible to get through without portaging; but be careful of your boat on the sharp bricks from the ruins of the aqueduct. If you climb up on to the bank you can see the remains of the high embankment which carried the canal on the north side of the river; on the other side it has vanished completely, ploughed up not much more than a hundred years after its creation.

Now Cricklade comes in sight, and you may think that the perils of your journey are at an end. But beware the hidden strands of barbed wire at the water's edge, which once punctured our inflatable dinghy. And take care of the 'gauging weir' at the foot of North Meadow, which has replaced the mill-shute at West Mill. It presents the boater with an unnerving downrush of water. Carry your craft round if you can, or let it slip down the right-hand slope. The weir measures the quantity of water coming down, and the measurement is passed on automatically to Thames Water Authority control points.

The meadows around here are good for camping (subject to the owner's permission). A short walk leads to the centre of Cricklade and an impressive number of pubs, giving the traveller ample opportunity to refresh himself before he continues his journey along the Thames.

# II

# The Navigation Begins: Cricklade to Buscot

SIGNS AND WONDERS

Cricklade Town Bridge bears on each side the inscription:
Rebuilt by the Feoffees
of the Cricklade Waylands
A.D. 1854

Henry Taunt (writing in the 1880s) explains: 'The good folk of Cricklade are blessed with a Waylands estate, which not only provides for the repair of the roads and pavements, but also lights up the streets with gas during the winter months without any rates to pay for it.' 'Feoffees' was the name given the estate trustees. The Waylands estate still exists, and still blesses the Cricklade residents. All profit from letting its land goes to defray the local rate.

Traffic thunders over Cricklade Town Bridge, but the inscription of the kindly feoffees is placed so that it can be read most easily from the river. Though few boats come here, Cricklade is by ancient tradition the head of navigation on the Thames. Thomas Baskervile in 1692 called it 'Cricklad the highest navigable place for Boats', and so it was for many years. Until the opening of the Thames & Severn Canal in 1789, small barges came here to load and unload. Now only canoes and rowing boats make Cricklade their terminus, but a man who can claim to be one of the strangest Thames travellers of recent times began his journey here.

On Christmas Eve, 1966, Alexander Wozniak, a Polish engineering draughtsman living in Dagenham, left Cricklade and set off down the river to walk *on* the water all the way to London, telling Press reporters that he was making the trip to celebrate 1,000 years of Christianity in Poland. He used 'skinoes', a cross between water-skis and canoes, designed to fit his feet. The *Swindon Evening Advertiser* reported: 'In the gathering dusk, he lost no time in donning his round safety floats before paddling to the river's edge in his skiff-like skinoes. A small crowd saw him disappear round a bend in the river.' Fortified by lemonade and vodka, Mr Wozniak splashed on through Christmas Day and five days following. At last, as Big Ben struck 10 a.m. on

Alexander Wozniak sets out from Cricklade on his 'skinoes' (*Swindon Evening Advertiser*).

The confluence of the Churn (top left) and Thames at Cricklade.

New Year's Eve, he arrived at Westminster Pier, where he said: 'I feel on top of the world.'

Even in a conventional boat, navigation is difficult for some miles below Cricklade. A few yards downstream of the Town Bridge, the Churn enters the Thames, bringing a substantial volume of water; but the river is still shallow in summer. Such deep stretches as occur are short and often choked with weed, so that it is impossible to use even a small outboard motor for long. In many places, particularly beneath the bridges, there are alarming rapids. Full-size launches should certainly not venture above Inglesham. This is not as much of a loss to the boater as might be expected: the banks are so high as to obscure all but a view of nearby cattle, caravans and modern houses. Evil-smelling clumps of weed float here in the summer, and this is the first place where people seem regularly to throw rubbish in the river. Plastic containers bob among the reeds; polythene bags, bottles and even oil-drums contribute to a sense that man has all too soon made his presence felt.

### KEMPSFORD AND THE HOUSE OF LANCASTER

At Castle Eaton, the Thames flows under a Victorian iron bridge more appropriate to a railway than to a river, and passes the Red Lion Inn. There is no towpath yet, but if you persevere you can meet the river at each village.

Downstream the next place of importance is Kempsford, a small village rapidly becoming a dormitory for Swindon. Its past was more splendid, for once the great John of Gaunt, 'time-honour'd Lancaster', had his castle where the vicarage garden now fronts the river. The fine perpendicular church tower was built by him in 1390 as a tribute to his first wife, Lady Blanche. The Lancaster family had many dealings with Geoffrey Chaucer, who wrote his poem 'The Book of the Duchesse' to commemorate the death of Lady Blanche in 1369. Chaucer almost certainly visited Kempsford; and there is a tradition that he composed some of his poetry here. Certainly it is easy to imagine him sitting on the ancient medlar tree by the river, in what is now the Vicar's garden, and composing lines like these, from his *The Parliament of Fowls*:

> A gardyn saw I ful of blosmy bowes
> Upon a ryver, in a grene mede,
> There as swetnesse evermore inow is,
> With flowres white, blewe, yelwe, and rede,
> And colde-welle stremes, nothyng dede,
> That swymmen ful of smale fishes lighte,
> With fynnes rede and skales sylver brighte.

At the foot of the vicarage garden is a grassy terrace called Lady Maud's

Kempsford church tower.

Walk, after the Duchess Blanche's sister. But the terrace was there long before
Lady Maud's day. It was originally made in Saxon times, when the Thames
formed the boundary between the kingdoms of Mercia and Wessex, to guard
the important ford which gave Kempsford its name. On 16 January A.D.
800, Ethelmund of the Hwiccians (who came from north of the Thames) rode
to the ford to attack the Wiltsaetas (the men of Wiltshire). The victory went

to the men of Wiltshire, and the hundred-acre meadow in which they fought is still called Battlefield. But nobody fords the river here now, and only the sparse ruins of a Jacobean house mark the site of John of Gaunt's castle.

This manor house stood at Kempsford until the end of the eighteenth century. But its owner at that time, Colonel George Hanger (later Lord Coleraine) was a member of the Prince Regent's fast-living set. He got into financial straits, was imprisoned for debt, and for a while earned his living as a coal merchant. He needed money so badly that he demolished the house at Kempsford and sold it for the value of the materials. Much of the stone was carried down the river by barge to help build the new mansion of the Lovedens at Buscot Park. George Hanger died in 1814, and with his death the fortunes of royalty ceased to affect the village of Kempsford.

Perhaps the strangest memorial of all to Kempsford's past glory is an old horseshoe nailed to the church door. Tradition has it that the first Duke of Lancaster's only son was drowned in the ford, which was peculiarly difficult to cross, and the duke was so grief-stricken that he rode from the village, never to return. His horse cast a shoe as it cantered out of Kempsford, and the villagers picked it up and nailed it to the church door for all to see.

### THE APPROACH TO LECHLADE

After Kempsford comes Hannington Bridge and its rapids; then a long remote stretch of river leading to Inglesham. On the right bank as you go downstream is Inglesham Church, built mainly in the late twelfth century; it is a perfect example of an unspoilt English village church which has escaped the excesses of Victorian 'restoration', and has most of its box pews intact as you would have seen them in the days of Queen Anne. The explanation is to be found on a copper plaque near the south door: 'This Church was repaired in 1888–9 through the energy and with the help of William Morris who loved it.' Morris lived at Kelmscott, only a few miles down river.

Almost opposite the church stands the 'round house' which marks the entrance to the disused Thames & Severn Canal. Here the River Coln flows into the Thames from its source in the Cotswolds and it is here also that the towpath begins, and the river becomes navigable for launches.

Lechlade is in sight, and the short stretch of river between the 'round house' and the town is busy in summer with cruisers and with skiffs hired from the Lechlade boatyard. Once Lechlade derived much of its income from the barge traffic, and now the pleasure boats and their crews bring revenue to the hotels, shops and cafes. A short distance below the town is St John's Lock, which is the highest on the Thames, and is named (like the bridge below it) after a priory which once stood nearby.

Inglesham Round House: the junction of the Thames, the Coln, and the Thames & Severn Canal.

### THE THAMES AND SEVERN CANAL

A little to the north of the river, from Cricklade to Inglesham, runs the line of the old Thames & Severn Canal which was opened in 1789.

It was abandoned in 1927, and along here little remains of it but the derelict locks and the strange 'round houses' where the lock keepers and watchmen lived. Often it is difficult to identify even the course the canal took; in some sections you can only find it by looking for the bridges.

The idea of connecting the Thames with the Severn was first conceived in the early years of the seventeenth century. Among the promoters of the project at this time was the first Earl Bathurst, and while staying with him at Cirencester Park in 1722 the poet Alexander Pope wrote of his patron's dream that the two rivers should 'celebrate their Marriage in the midst of an immense Amphitheatre'. But it was not until the 1780s that a company began to construct a canal linking the Thames and Severn. The outline planning was done by Robert Whitworth, a pupil of the great canal builder James Brindley, but the engineer with direct responsibility for the construction was Josiah Clowes. The canal left the Thames at Inglesham and progressed upwards by means of sixteen locks until it reached the summit level at Coates; here it ran beneath the hill through the long Sapperton Tunnel, emerging at Daneway to climb steeply down the Golden Valley to Walbridge. Thence, as the Stroudwater Navigation, it ran alongside the River Frome to Saul Junction, where it crossed the Gloucester and Berkeley Ship Canal, and emerged into the Severn estuary. The locks on the Thames & Severn were, when the canal was first opened, about ninety feet long and a little over twelve feet wide. In the lower part of the Golden Valley they were a little wider, to fit the Severn trows which traded to Brimscombe; but Thames barges could be accommodated along the whole length of the canal.

There was much trade on the canal in the early days. Goods taken to the company's wharf in London in 1793 were principally tin, iron from Coalbrookdale, cider, copper, lead, salt, cheese, brass, groceries, rags, tallow, dye-woods, potash and oil. Commodities carried in smaller quantities included: puncheons of perry; sugar in lumps, loaves, bags and hogsheads; carrotels of currants; firkins of butter; bobbins of flax; pockets and bags of hops; sticks of timber; and casks of purgative squills. But even in the early days the trade tended to be of a one-way nature: there were fewer commodities to bring back from London, and often the company's boats remained many days at Hambro Wharf before they could get a full load for the return trip. Then, all too soon, there came competition.

For twenty-five years the canal's mainstay was Staffordshire coal from Bilston. It came in narrow boats from the Birmingham canals to Stourport, where it was transhipped into trows and carried along the Stroudwater to Brimscombe in the Golden Valley; there it was sold locally or transhipped yet again and sent further east in Thames barges. This may seem a long and tortuous route, but in the 1790s the Thames & Severn and the Oxford Canal formed the only water links between London and the Midlands coalfields. Then in 1800 the Grand Junction Canal opened from London to Braunston; and this, together with its connecting canals, formed a completely new and much shorter route to Birmingham. The importance of the Thames & Severn as a trunk route was considerably diminished.

After this date there was still plenty of traffic on the Thames & Severn, but it was to be found principally in the Golden Valley section west of the tunnel, where boats traded extensively between the Severn and Brimscombe. Fewer and fewer came over the summit to the Thames; by 1839 an average of only six boats a day were passing Sapperton Tunnel—a pitifully small number when one considers the cost of maintaining the canal. Indeed, maintenance was becoming a more severe problem than lack of traffic: the summit-level leaked badly, and there was a constant shortage of water. The pumping station at Thames Head was set up, but water levels remained low, especially in the summer, so that boats often had to unload part of their cargo and travel light to avoid grounding. This too discouraged trade.

Then came railway competition. The Great Western Railway opened its main line from London to Bristol in 1841; in the same year a branch line to Cirencester began to operate; and only four years later the main line to Gloucester was opened from a junction at Swindon. The canal company's revenue fell swiftly, for railway transport was quicker and often cheaper (the Thames & Severn was having to charge heavy tolls to offset its costs). Meantime the G.W.R. had its own interest in the canal, not as a watercourse but as the line of a projected railway from Stroud to Cirencester, and eventually in 1882 the railway bought a controlling interest in the Thames & Severn Canal's shares. By this time the canal was a dying concern: no dividend had been paid to shareholders since 1864. In 1893 it was announced that the canal would be closed east of Chalford, leaving only the lower section which connected with the Stroudwater, and preventing through traffic from reaching the tunnel and the Thames. Strong opposition to this closure eventually resulted in the formation of the Thames & Severn Canal Trust, which acquired the canal from the G.W.R. in 1895, and reopened it throughout its length in 1899. But the summit was not watertight, and navigation ceased after only a few months. In despair the Trust asked Gloucestershire County Council to take over the waterway; the Council complied, launching into what the *Gloucester Journal* called 'a daring adventure into the realm of Municipal socialism'. It would have been more accurate to call it a rash squandering of ratepayers' money: during the succeeding years £64,000 was spent trying to restore and operate the canal, but to no avail. Braithwaite and Co. of Leeds 'repuddled' the summit-level with a new clay lining, but they did the job badly with lumpy, poorly mixed clay. Others took over, and the canal was reopened in 1904, but the work was of an insufficiently high standard (the old techniques had been forgotten) and water still ran away down holes and fissures. Pleasure craft began to use the canal, including *Flower of Gloster* with the writer E. Temple Thurston on board (his book, named after the boat and still available, is a wonderful account of canal travel in those days); but there were no more than half a dozen pleasure boats a year and very few trading craft. There was virtually no revenue from tolls (as early as 1881 the total revenue for the year from this source was a mere £3 6s 10d) and closure was inevitable. The section east of the Golden Valley was eventually abandoned on 31 January 1927; the Stroudwater struggled on for twenty years more, but at last it too succumbed.

Today a number of Britain's derelict canals are being restored or considered for restoration, and the Thames & Severn has not been neglected. In 1972 the Stroudwater Canal Society was formed with the aim of restoring navigation to the Stroudwater and Thames & Severn Canals. Though the task would seem herculean, the Society says that 'support locally is phenomenal and membership is increasing'.

The full story of the canal can be found in *The Thames & Severn Canal* by Humphrey Household (1969), a book which also provides much incidental information about the Thames.

## BASKERVILE'S TRAVELS

In 1692 Matthew Thomas Baskervile, 'Master of Bayworth House' at Sunningwell near Abingdon, wrote an account of 'Bridges over y^e famous River Tems' from Cricklade to Wallingford. The description is contained, together with some of the author's household accounts, several passages of verse, and a list of London taverns, in a manuscript now housed in the British Museum (Harleian MS 4716). The verses are an account of a journey Baskervile made down the Thames in his sixty-second year. He set out from Cricklade, and if he intended to make Wallingford his goal for his journey as well as for the catalogue of bridges, then he was apparently soon distracted (perhaps by taverns) and never reached his destination. But that part of the journey he accomplished inspired him to write some most entertaining verse and prose. Here is his departure from Cricklade.

> So farwell Cricklad, come of y^t ground,
> We'el sail in Boats, towards London Town,
> Ffor this now is, the highest station,
> By famous Tems for Navigation,
> But when th 'tis joyn'd with Bath Avon,
> Then row your wherrys farther on,
> ffor Baskervile, Matthews were Projectors,
> How to do it since Lords Protectors,
> Who did conclude, sixty thousand pound,
> Would thoroughly open, each river ground,
> ffor by power of Lakes, Rains, & ffountains,
> They'l make Boats to dance, upon y^e mountains.

This refers to the projected North Wilts Canal, which later did indeed link the Thames with the Bath Avon. Baskervile eventually reaches Hannington Bridge and describes it in prose, noting that 'Mr ffreak lives at Hannington'. He continues:

> But I'le return, our Boats move on,
> We'r come to bridge of Hannington

25

> So, here if any are now dry
> Here's Ale to quench your thirst hard by,
> In sixteen hundred ninety tow,
> Saunders made Ale, to serve the crew.

Saunders' Alehouse vanished long ago and there is—alas—no inn at Hannington now.

Eventually Baskervile reaches Lechlade, and gives us a good account of the river traffic to be found there in his day:

> I have seen 6 or 8 boats togeither at their Wharfe. For besides Corn of all sorts, which they lade to go down stream, here comes from Severn and Avon, landed at Tewxbury (where both those Rivers do unite) and elsewhere, on horses and in carts & wagons by land, great weights of Cheese, especially that sort gos by y^e name of Cheshier Cheese. For here about the Boates Masters have warehouses to serve their goods. And hops in times of scarcity, & other goods, comes from London-ward hether, & are sent (as aforesaid) by land to Severn, and thence in Boats to Bristol and elswere, & in ships to Ireland.

Baskervile now moves on to St John's Bridge, a short distance below Lechlade, and describes the fair which he found there:

> St John Bridge fair is kept on the 29 day of August in the Meadow below y^e bridge on Glocestershire side, to which Oxford boats & others resort to sell Ale, Beef & Carrots, & to carry goods from this fair down stream . . . It is a great fair for Cattle & Cheese, & here you meet with brave sage cheese no place elswere in England shews the like, much diversified in figures, green and white, as to round chees, and some in shape of Dolphins & Mermaids, as Countrey Carvers display them in Cheesfats.

He goes on in verse:

> The fair is done, each maid is kist
> So I crave leave to be dismist,
> Away they ride, trot run and go
> As fast as in the morn they flo
> So over bridge I'le gallop after
> And search about for other water
> And here I find a stream divides
> Sweet Berkshier from y^e Wiltshire side
> Which makes an Ile or watry ham
> between Buscot and Inglesham
> And in Buscot I understand

Dwells a Captain of our trainbands
Master Loveden is his name
A person of good worth and fame
Long may he live in wealth and honour
With a kind lass to tumble on her.


## THE BARGE TRAFFIC

Lechlade is by long tradition the highest point to which the full sized Thames barges came; at certain stages in the river's history smaller craft penetrated to Cricklade and even perhaps to Ashton Keynes, but Lechlade was and is the head of navigation for boats of any size.

The Romans and probably the ancient Britons before them used the Thames for carrying merchandise, and this practice continued extensively until the middle of the nineteenth century and to a lesser degree into the twentieth. Water transport was for many centuries cheaper and easier than the hard passage by unmetalled roads. Sometimes the river was used to carry large quantities of a single commodity, such as the Taynton stone Sir Christopher Wren arranged to ship from Newbridge to London for the rebuilding of St Paul's. More often the barges carried a miscellany of goods. A Lechlade bargemaster stated in 1793 that the chief goods he carried down to London were: 'Iron, Copper, Tin, manufactured and pig Iron, Brass, Spelter, Cannon, Cheese, Nails, all Iron goods and Bomb Shells.' The iron had probably come from the Midlands by way of the Thames & Severn Canal. From London this same bargemaster brought back to Lechlade 'Groceries, Deals, Foreign Timber, Merchandise of every Kind, a few Coals, and of late Raw Hides for Tewkesbury and Worcester and Gunpowder to Bristol and Liverpool'. (The latter would certainly have continued their journey via the canal.)

As to the boats themselves, there was no single pattern; it all depended on the whim of the boatbuilder and the need of the bargemaster. The average Thames barge in the eighteenth century was flat bottomed (a very necessary feature, as the boat had to be able to lie on the shallows without coming to harm); its sides were almost vertical, or perhaps slightly rounded, and it had square ends which sloped up like a punt; a rudder hung from a projecting fin. There was no proper deck or cabin, and the crew sheltered under a canvas awning at the stern. There was generally one sail, a simple square affair on a central mast, and the mast itself was hinged so that it could be lowered to pass under bridges. Later, fore and aft sails were introduced, set by a spit or by gaff and boom. The size and capacity of the barges varied greatly: craft are recorded with burdens from eight to 200 tons, but the

Thames barge, 1811.

average was between sixty and 130 tons. A sixty ton barge would be about eighty-five feet long and twelve feet wide, with a draught of four feet.

Propulsion of the Thames barges was by various means. If the sail was hoisted it would, with sufficient wind, provide adequate motive power in straight broad stretches of the river where tacking was possible. But in the upper reaches where the river winds a narrow course, and in the lower reaches when there was no wind, some other means had to be found. Towing was frequently used, either in conjunction with or instead of the sail. The tow line was attached not to the bow of the barge (that would have dragged the vessel towards the bank) but to the top of the mast, where it had less influence on the steering and was high enough to pass over obstacles on the bank. The towing was done by men or horses. In the early days men were often used; they were called 'halers' and were probably recruited locally as casual labour when the barge passed through an inhabited area. Halers were regarded as the roughest sort of men, and were generally much feared along the river. Enormous numbers of them were needed to drag a fully laden boat over the shallows: it was said of the Thames in 1730 that 'upwards of Three Score Men are now employed to each Barge to tow it, when six Horses might be sufficient for that purpose'. Horses did supersede men in time, so that by the nineteenth century the use of halers seems to have ceased; but even the leading of towing-horses could be difficult, and the lad appointed to do the job would often have to wade up to his waist in water in places where the towpath had eroded. These, then, were the principal means of haulage; but when conditions got bad and motive power was short the bargemen resorted to the simplest method of getting along—punting the

28

A Thames barge in the early nineteenth century, with sail and towing horses.

boat with poles.

It is difficult to get a full picture of life on the Thames barges before the nineteenth century. Records are sparse, partly because bargemasters on the Upper River were not required to register their craft or crew. But local documents give us occasional glimpses. The town records of Abingdon describe at the end of the eighteenth century a barge called *The True Briton*; she was of 122 tons burden, had a master, one man as 'Steersman and Costbearer' (this meant that he had responsibility for paying lock tolls and handing out wages to the halers), four men as bargemen and navigators, and a boy to do errands. At the same date the *Toll Dish*, also of Abingdon and of forty-five tons, had three men as crew. The bargemasters (as the owners of these vessels were always called) seem to have varied in status and affluence. Some, such as perhaps the master of the *True Briton*, were land based merchants who operated several barges, maybe as only one part of their business. Others were working bargemen who steered their own boat, or were partners in it (this seems to have been the status of the three man crew of the *Toll Dish*).

Like the canal boatmen later on, the Thames bargemen attracted a good deal of abuse. They were held to be 'seldom of the better sort . . . but a fewe dronken and beggerley fellows' (1600); another writer, in the eighteenth century, explained that 'they use singular and quite extraordinary terms, and generally very coarse and dirty ones, and I cannot explain them to you'. Bargemen must by the nature of their job have been a tough lot, but perhaps the fairest verdict on them comes from a seventeenth-century pamphlet: 'I know many water-men, and I know them to be like other men, some very honest men, and some knaves.'

29

If you want to use a boat on the Thames, you must first register it with the Thames Water Authority, and pay an annual registration fee. This process is descended from an ancient system of toll collection on the river, a system which fettered the boat traffic for many years.

In the earliest days, the Thames was free of artificial obstructions. But as soon as men began to build mills, engage in organised fishing, or attempt navigation with large boats, the use of weirs became advantageous. They penned in the water and controlled its level, to the benefit of miller, fishermen and navigator. But the weirs on the Thames were not established according to any organised plan: they were generally set up by a miller or a local squire, who soon acquired the right to levy a toll from all boats passing his weir. Gradually, pound locks with top and bottom gates were introduced to replace the weirs, but once again a toll was payable for passing them. Navigation became an expensive business: in the mid-eighteenth century there were twenty-five locks and weirs between Lechlade and Oxford, each one charging a toll varying from 1s to 2s 6d per boat. But this was a trifle compared to the cost of a river journey between Oxford and London at the same date. Below Oxford tolls were levied at thirty-two places (including some bridges), and this toll varied from 1s to 35s, the average being about 10s. In 1791 the master of a sixty ton barge paid £26 16s 10d in tolls between Lechlade and London. The enormous cost of such journeys, coupled with long delays while the barges waited for the weirs to be opened, sounded the death knell of profitable commercial carrying on the Upper Thames.

To make matters worse, at the end of the eighteenth century there came competition from the newly built canals. At first the Thames played an important part in the new network of waterways, providing a passage by water from London to the Midlands and Bristol, via the Oxford Canal and the Thames & Severn Canal. But in 1800 the Grand Junction Canal was opened, providing an independent route from London to Birmingham and the coalfields, and bypassing the Thames. Then the railways arrived, eventually serving all places of importance along the river. Railway transport was quicker and easier than river carrying, and thanks to the pernicious tolls on the Thames it was generally cheaper. Barge traffic on the river was reduced to a fraction of what it had been; the traditional Thames barge with its tall mast and punt-like shape soon disappeared, leaving the residual trade to the ubiquitous narrow boats which had crept into the river from the canal system.

In 1866 the Thames Conservancy was given powers to govern the whole river from Cricklade to Yantlet Creek. One of its first actions was to replace the old tolls with a properly regulated system of levies. All boats had to be registered (in 1887 the registration fee for a private pleasure boat was 2s 6d per annum) and in addition a toll had to be paid at each lock or weir; but the new tolls were standardized, and generally lower than the old ones. Rowing boats paid from 3d to 1s depending on their size, while steam launches were let through for 1s 6d. Perhaps even more important, over the succeeding years the Conservancy removed most of the old navigation weirs and replaced them where necessary with pound locks. But by then, trade had almost completely disappeared from the river above Oxford, and the chief benefit of the improvements was felt by the growing number of pleasure-boaters.

It should not be supposed that the Thames before the 1860s was the only waterway that charged high tolls: its neighbour the Thames & Severn Canal was notorious for the high levy it imposed on boaters. Though the canal was undoubtedly one of the most beautiful in the country, the Company resolutely opposed its use by pleasure-boaters, making things as expensive for them as it could. In the summer of 1815 the poet Percy Bysshe Shelley, with his future wife Mary and two friends, arrived at Inglesham intending to row along the Thames & Severn Canal and then up the Severn. To their dismay they found that the use of the canal would cost them £20, as much as if they were the crew of a sixty ton barge. They did not make the journey.

ST JOHN'S LOCK TO KELMSCOTT

Nearly a mile downstream of St John's Lock, the river runs close to the A417 main road. Here, on a grassy clearing now owned by the National Trust, stood the old warehouses where (according to Henry Taunt) cheese and corn were brought from upstream by small craft and transhipped into larger barges for London and elsewhere. Traces of brickwork can still be seen here.

Shortly below this on the same side of the river stand Buscot Church and the accompanying Queen Anne rectory (also the property of the National Trust). In Buscot Church is buried the Master Loveden mentioned by Thomas Baskervile. The Lovedens lived at nearby Buscot Park, which remained in their family until 1859. It was then bought by Robert Campbell, a gentleman of colonial origins, who engaged in a rather peculiar form of commerce inspired by the large crop of beetroot which grew on the estate. Henry Taunt wrote in the 1880s: 'Buscot Lock . . . Just before reaching here we pass the immense factory where spirit was made from beetroot; the manufacture not being successful has been given up and the factory entirely taken down.' Squire Campbell died in 1887, and Buscot Park was bought by the man who was made the first Earl of Faringdon. Now the house has been donated to the National Trust, although the present Lord Faringdon still lives there.

'Pill-box' at Buscot.

Any journey along this stretch of the river is made under the eyes of 'pill-boxes', the strange squat concrete huts that stand guard on so many of the river's vantage points. They were built in the early days of the Second World War as a defence against a possible water-borne invasion. Originally they were camouflaged with chicken feathers stuck to wire netting, and must have looked a strange sight. Cows rubbed against them, and the feathers soon came off. Too well-built and solid to be demolished with ease, the pill-boxes have stayed, largely useless, but perhaps now beginning the journey from eyesore to ancient monument.

# III

# The Upper River: Buscot to Oxford

Buscot Weir (standing by Buscot Lock) is one of the finest of the old weirs on the Thames. It is also easily accessible if you want to take a close look at it. Weirs like this played an influential and fascinating part in the history of the river.

Until Saxon times rivers were probably free of artificial obstructions. Then mills and fisheries developed, and with them came weirs. Millers needed weirs to pen up the water and provide sufficient power to turn the mill-wheel. Fishery owners (often monasteries) found that excellent catches could be obtained from fishing weirs and eel traps set across the river.

Weirs could be a great nuisance. As they grew in number they caused floods, spoilt the fishing for other people, and hindered the passage of boats. But in one way they did help the navigation. Rivers in their natural state have many shallows or 'shoals' where the water flows fast and furious and provides little floating depth. Strategically positioned weirs raise the water level and make navigation possible over these shallows.

But the boats had to get through the weirs. This was done on the Thames by making a central portion of the weir removable. A heavy wooden beam was laid in the river bed, usually fixed in a masonry 'sill'. A similar beam was positioned over it, above the surface of the water. This second beam was secured to the bank or to a fixed part of the weir, but it could be swung aside or otherwise removed. Next, a number of squared vertical timbers called 'rymers' were fixed at intervals into sockets in the lower beam, so that they rested against the upstream side of the upper beam, and were held in position by the current. Finally, against the rymers there rested a series of boards attached to long wooden handles, holding back the water, and called 'paddles'.

When a boat was to pass the weir, first the paddles were withdrawn one by one. Then the rymers were taken out. Finally the upper beam was pulled or swung out of the way. Immediately following the opening of the weir there

Medley Weir in the 1920s. In the upper picture the weir is shut. In the lower the rymers and paddles have been removed from one half, the beam has been swung aside, and a launch is 'flashing' through (*R. R. Bolland* collection).

Radcot Weir in the early 1800s.

would be a great downrush of water. Barges going downstream would shoot the weir as soon as it was practicable, and the flush or 'flash' of water helped to carry them over the shallows in the reach below. Barges going upstream would wait for the rush of water to subside a little, and they would then be hauled through the opening (either by a winch, a gang of men, or a team of horses).

Weirs like this were in use for many centuries, and a large number of them (especially on the Upper Thames) continued to exist long after the introduction of locks as we know them. Four of these 'flash weirs', as they were generally called, survived even into the present century (those at Medley, King's, Eynsham and Eaton Hastings). The last to remain in existence, Medley Weir, was not removed until 1937.

Weirs often adjoined mills, since it was the mills that had been partly responsible for creating the need for them. When the miller opened the weir, the amount of water available to turn his wheel was substantially reduced. So millers were unwilling to let barges 'flash' through except at times—and prices—that suited them. Consequently tolls at weirs became heavy, and there were frequent disputes between millers and bargemen. Vessels would sometimes be held up for days if the water level was low and the miller refused to draw the weir.

A good description of 'flashing' down a weir in the 1870s is provided by Henry Taunt, writing about his experiences at Eaton Hastings. In this case

The footbridge and Anchor Inn on the site of the weir at Eaton Hastings.

the boat was small (a gig) and so the upper beam was not removed.

> In winter there is a swift stream through, but very little fall . . .
> and the only thing to guard against in shooting is the bridge that
> carries the rymers. I recollect one winter in passing this very weir,
> when lying on my back in the boat to get through, scraping a
> fair amount of skin off my nose and face, through contact with
> the bridge whilst going under. In summer there is no fear of that,
> as the bridge is a long way above the water, but what must be
> looked out for is the nearly direct fall of a foot or more in ascend-
> ing or descending . . . It is always the better, if you have not been
> through before, to get help from the neighbouring cottage, refresh-
> ing yourself if needed; and a small quantity of the Englishman's
> *bucksheesh* (beer) will always find you a willing assistant.

Buscot Weir looks very much as it did in Taunt's day, although boats no
longer 'flash' through, but use the adjacent lock. The rymers and paddles
are still removed and replaced, purely to control the water level. This
laborious task (a rymer weighs nearly 100 lbs) is undertaken by the lock
keeper, sometimes in the middle of the night in bitter weather. For this
reason many of the old rymer and paddle weirs have been replaced by mech-
anically operated sluices. But it is to be hoped that the Thames Water
Authority will allow at least a few of the old weirs to remain as examples.
The lock keepers say they would be sorry to see them go.

Many weirs were known by the names of their keepers. Eaton Hastings Weir (about a mile below Buscot) was often called Hart's, from the name of the family who kept it for at least a hundred years. A footbridge now marks its site, and the Anchor Inn stands where Henry Taunt obtained *bucksheesh* from the weirkeeper's cottage. Footbridges also mark the sites of Ten Foot, Old Man's and Ridge's near Northmoor. Other weirs have left no trace but the memory of their names: Old Nan's, Winney Weg's, Noah's Ark, Skinner's.

At Ridge's (near Northmoor) Betty, the weirkeeper's daughter, caught the eye of a young peer rowing by. He had her educated, and married her at Northmoor Church in 1766. Thus she became Lady Pencot, and was much loved and respected in the locality. The name 'Pencots' is still given to a group of houses in the village.

Many weirs had inns attached. At Skinner's, a little below Bablock Hythe, stood The Fish. Taunt wrote of it: 'It was a little inn; and the last landlord, Joe Skinner, was one of the best-hearted, quaintest fellows that ever lived. He was original in the highest degree, and it was a rich treat to listen to his curious remarks on some one who, not understanding him, had rubbed old Joe the wrong way of the wool.'

CHLORAL AND ASPARAGUS

Kelmscott is almost opposite Eaton Hastings. A few fields separate the village from the river, and it is possible to pass downstream without catching more than a glimpse of its grey stone houses half hidden behind the screen of trees. But do not miss the chance to visit it, for here lived a man who loved and wrote much about the Thames above Oxford. And here too were played out some strange scenes.

In 1871 William Morris was searching for a summer retreat for his family, who were then living in Bloomsbury. He saw an advertisement that Kelmscott Manor was to let. He wrote: 'I have been looking about for a house for the wife and kids, and whither do you guess my eye is turned now? Kelmscott, a little village about two miles above Radcott Bridge—a heaven on earth; an old stone Elizabethan house like Water Eaton, and such a garden close down on the river, a boat house and all things handy. I am going down there again on Saturday with Rossetti and my wife· Rossetti because he thinks of sharing it with us if the thing looks likely.' Morris was already well established as a writer, artist, decorator, manufacturer and printer. Dante Gabriel Rossetti, a founder member of the Pre-Raphaelite Brotherhood, had become known for his poems as well as for his work as an artist.

These two travelled to Kelmscott with Morris's wife Jane, the beautiful

Kelmscott Manor.

daughter of an Oxford livery-stable keeper. They decided to take the house, Morris and Rossetti sharing the rent of sixty pounds a year.

The Manor (originally a small farmhouse, enlarged in the seventeenth century) was utterly to Morris's liking. But Rossetti soon found life there unbearably dull. He wrote in 1871 that the surrounding country was 'deadly flat', the river-walks pretty but 'somewhat monotonous', and the village 'the doziest clump of old beehives to look at that you could find anywhere'. Meanwhile he was not helping his condition by the large doses of chloral (a popular Victorian sleeping draught) which he took nightly, washed down with whisky, to help his insomnia. He and Morris could scarcely live in the same house. Rossetti went to bed at 3 or 4 a.m., Morris would rise at 5 or 6 to begin a strenuous day's work. Rossetti would eventually get up from his drugged sleep to take a late breakfast and make sarcastic remarks about the house or whatever task Morris was engaged in. To make matters worse, Rossetti was infatuated with Jane Morris. Her wide-set eyes, full mouth and fine dark hair appear in many of his canvasses, and though the nature of his passion for her is hard to define, he certainly saw her as more than artist's model.

William Morris, by G. F. Watts, 1880 (*National Portrait Gallery*).

Morris was often away from Kelmscott, either in London or abroad. But though Rossetti was able to spend much time there with his beloved Janey, his condition did not improve. In London he tried to commit suicide by taking an overdose of chloral; he recovered and returned to Kelmscott, but only remained there until 1874. In the summer of that year he was walking by the Thames with his friend George Hake when he heard, or thought he heard, a party of fishermen make an insulting remark about him. He turned on the men and showered them with abuse. Hake tried to smooth things over, but there had in any case been a good deal of local gossip about the *ménage à trois* at the Manor, and it was thought best that Rossetti should leave, resigning his joint tenancy. He went back to London and lived in Cheyne Walk; his addiction to chloral continued, and he died in 1882, aged 54.

Rossetti's portrait of Jane Morris
as *Proserpine*, 1874 (*Tate Gallery*).

Now Morris had Kelmscott to himself. He visited it often and with great delight. Here are a few extracts from his letters written at the Manor: 'I never yet till now understood how green the grass could be in spring; it is so green that it brings all the distance near and flattens the landscape into a medieval picture . . . It has just been raining May butter, as Izaak Walton says: looked for an hour as if it would never stop raining again; then it got a little lighter, and then of a sudden was the bright sun and a rainbow. Item, I have eaten asparagus and heard the cuckoo: the blackbirds wake me about 4 o'clock a.m.: as for the rooks they never stop all day long.'

Dante Rossetti, a
self portrait (*National
Portrait Gallery*).

In 1878 Morris moved his London home to Hammersmith, where he had
found a house on the Upper Mall by the river. He called it Kelmscott House,
and liked to think that the Thames water which flowed past its windows had
flowed also past Kelmscott Manor in the meadows 130 miles up the stream.
In the summer of 1880 he made his first river voyage from Hammersmith to
Kelmscott, with his family, in a boat called the *Ark*. He wrote of the vessel:
'She is old but delightful: imagine a biggish company boat with a small
omnibus on board, fitted up luxuriously inside with shelves and a glass-rack,
and a sort of boot behind this: room for two rowers in front, and I must say
for not many more except in the cabin or omnibus. Still what a joy (to a little
mind) to see the landscape out of a square pane of glass, and to sleep a-nights
with the stream rushing two inches past one's ear.' The journey went well,
with Morris often doing the cooking. Eventually they reached Oxford and
the Upper River:

We got up early and by dint of great exertions started from Medley Lock at 9 a.m., with Bossom and another man to tow us as far as New Bridge, where we sent them off, and muddled ourselves home somehow, dining at a lovely place about a mile above New Bridge, where I have stopped before for that end. One thing was very pleasant: they were haymaking on the flat flood-washed spits of ground and islets all about Tadpole; and the hay was gathered on punts and the like; odd stuff to look at, mostly sedge, but they told us it was the best of stuff for milk.

Night fell on us long before we got to Radcot, and we fastened a lantern to the prow of our boat, after we had with much difficulty got our boats through Radcot Bridge. Charles was waiting us with a lantern at our bridge by the corner at 10 p.m., and presently the ancient house had me in its arms again.

William Morris died in 1896 at Hammersmith: he was buried at Kelmscott. The Hammersmith house was sold and Jane retired to Kelmscott (which the family eventually came to own), remaining their until her death in 1914. Their daughter May lived there, carrying on the tradition of Pre-Raphaelite craftsmanship, until her own death in 1938. The house contains many relics of the family and the Pre-Raphaelite movement, and is open to the public for one day each month.


## RADCOT BRIDGE

From Kelmscott it is nearly two miles by water to Grafton Lock; then another mile and the river divides. A sign directs boats to take the left-hand channel going downstream, and this leads to an eighteenth-century single-arched bridge. A journey down the right-hand channel (still navigable by small craft) is much more rewarding, for spanning this stream is a much older bridge, with three fine mediæval arches. It is probably the oldest bridge on the Thames.

As early as A.D. 958 there was, according to a Saxon charter, a bridge of stone in this vicinity. (See Birch, *Cartularium Saxonicum*, iii. 228.) If the Saxon bridge was at Radcot, its foundations may have been retained under the present bridge, whose masonry piers are said to date from the twelfth century or earlier. The two outer pointed arches may (according to Nikolaus Pevsner) be fourteenth century; the centre arch is definitely later.

It is conceivable that the present bridge was originally built (perhaps with three identical ribbed and pointed arches) after the events of 1387. In that year Robert de Vere, Earl of Oxford, Duke of Ireland and a favourite of Richard II, was fleeing from Bolingbroke's troops. He arrived at a place

Radcot Bridge.

which seems to have been Radcot, where he found the bridge broken down by his enemies. (He eventually escaped by fording the river on horseback.)

Clearly Radcot Bridge has been repaired several times in its history. In 1512 the Patent Rolls (6 Edward II, i. 8) record a grant of Pontage 'for the repair of the bridge of Radecote'. (Pontage was a toll exacted for the maintenance of bridges.) Perhaps it was at this date that the original middle arch was widened to allow larger boats to pass through. This centre arch (which now has no ribs) does not seem to have been constructed entirely successfully: the stonework has shifted a little from its original position, and at some date tie rods were inserted into the northern arch to strengthen the bridge.

The bridge is built of stone from Taynton Quarry, about ten miles to the north of Radcot.* Stone has been quarried there for at least a thousand years, and was used in the building of many Oxford colleges. One of the great advantages of Taynton stone seems to have been that it could be delivered cheaply by river. It seems that sometimes it was transported on rafts down the Windrush to that river's confluence with the Thames at Newbridge, and thence down to Oxford. At other times it was brought by cart to Radcot (the nearest convenient wharf on the Thames itself) and there loaded on to barges.

* We have this on the authority of Mr Harry Kimber and Mr Stan Day, two masons with wide experience of the various varieties of stone quarried in the locality.

43

Tadpole Bridge.

Taynton stone also went further down the river, below Oxford. In the fourteenth century it was used for building at Windsor Castle, and three hundred years later it played an important part in Sir Christopher Wren's reconstruction of London after the Great Fire. One of Wren's master masons, Thomas Strong, owned Taynton Quarry. The neighbouring Upton Quarry at Burford was owned by Christopher Kempster, who also worked for Wren. Both men naturally used their own stone, and Kempster's day-book shows that Radcot was in consequence the scene of much activity:

> September 20, 1672. Then loaded into Houses boat 8 tunn 3 foot ffrom ratcat . . . September 21. Then was loaded into Humphry Duffins boat 75 ffoot of ston at ratcat . . . September 26. Then was loaded into Houses boat 9 tunn two foot ffrom ratcat pd. him then fivety shillings.

Radcot Bridge is unusual in having 'splitwaters' on both its upstream and downstream sides. These v-shaped piers were an essential feature of mediæval bridge-building, as they prevented the current from striking the masonry with too great a force and washing away the mortar. On the upstream side splitwaters are functional; at Newbridge they are found on the upstream side alone. Downstream, as at Radcot, they are purely for the sake of symmetry. Above the central arch on the east side is a pedestal which once held an ornament, perhaps a stone cross.

In 1787 an artificial 'cut' or canal was made at Radcot to take the navigation on its present course, north of the old bridge and nearer to the Swan

44

Tenfoot Bridge.

Hotel. This was an 'improvement' made in anticipation of increased traffic from the new Thames & Severn Canal. But the 'cut' has more bends than the old course of the river, and the newer bridge with its single arch (also built of Taynton stone) lies askew the channel and presents a hazard to boats. It was probably this bridge that William Morris had 'much difficulty' in getting through on his journey from Hammersmith.

### FORD AND FERRY

From Radcot to Shifford is the most remote and in some ways the loveliest stretch of the Upper River. There are no roads or railways even distantly in sight or sound, and the only houses are at Rushey Lock and Tadpole Bridge. This bridge, with its single arch, and roundels and keystones in relief, was constructed in the late eighteenth century, and here too the stone is thought to come from Taynton. Why 'Tadpole' no one can say for certain. The Trout Inn stands by; despite the huge pylons a few hundred yards away, it is not supplied with mains electricity, but generates its own, and uses gas lighting. Over the door there once were the words: 'The Trout, kept by A. Herring'.

The river winds on through remote meadows. Tenfoot Bridge (the site of an old flash weir which perhaps had an opening ten feet wide) is the only landmark until the little hamlet of Chimney appears on the north bank. Here

45

Newbridge.

the navigation takes a straight course through Shifford Lock Cut, dug in 1896–7 to avoid a big meander. But the old course of the river should not be ignored; walk across the fields to Duxford, where you can still ford the Thames on foot, as people have done here for many centuries. Shifford itself is only a tiny village, but it was important enough in Saxon times for Alfred to hold a parliament here.

And then comes Newbridge, popularly supposed to be the oldest bridge on the river, but probably a little' younger than Radcot Bridge. Perhaps it was 'new' in comparison with Radcot? Here all six mediæval pointed arches are intact, here too the stone came from Taynton, and here again it is impossible to say exactly when the bridge was built. Thacker suggests that 1250 was the date of the original bridge, and that it was rebuilt in the middle of the fifteenth century.

John Leland came here in Henry VIII's time, and wrote that it was 'fayre champayne ground, frutefull of corne . . . The ground ther al about lyethe in low medowes often ovarflowne by rage of reyne . . . The bridge it selfe hathe vi. greate arches of stone.'

Leaving Newbridge and its two inns (the Maybush and the Rose Revived, each with its own attractions) the river begins the northward sweep which will take it around the Cumnor landmass. Abingdon is now six miles away as the crow flies, but twenty-two miles by water. After the footbridge marking the site of Ridge's Weir (also known as Hart's), we pass Northmoor Lock and come to Bablock Hythe.

46

Bablock Hythe Ferry circa 1885 (*Henry Taunt*).

Thomas Baskervile wrote in 1692: 'Bablock Hythe has a great boat to carry over Carts and Coaches', and in fact there was a ferry operating here until quite recently. Once there were dozens of ferries like it on the river; their principal function was to carry towing-horses across when the path changed sides, but they were also important for local traffic. In the present century the Bablock Hythe ferry carried motor cars, but in the mid 1960s it became unsafe and eventually ceased to operate; now only the winch and the supports for the cable remain.

Although the ferry boat has gone, the Chequers Inn here has been renamed The Ferry, and is the focal point for an uncompromising riverside development. Caravans used as holiday homes line the water's edge, while another site a little further back from the river provides permanent accommodation in larger caravan-type dwellings. The place has changed a good deal since Mathew Arnold called it 'retired ground' in his poem 'The Scholar-Gipsy':

> Thee at the ferry Oxford riders blithe,
> Returning home on summer-nights, have met
> Crossing the stripling Thames at Bab-lock-hithe,
> Trailing in the cool stream thy fingers wet,
> As the punt's rope chops round.

Despite the caravans, there are still remote and quiet corners here. You can walk along the wooded path on the Cumnor bank and look out for the old Physic Well hidden in the trees, or go on foot to Northmoor and search for both its inns.


UNDER CANVAS

Bablock Hythe is a good place to stay the night, particularly if you are camping; the people at the inn will let you pitch your tent by the site of the old ferry. Or perhaps you will be lucky enough to be travelling in one of the few remaining 'camping boats', a punt or skiff with a canvas cover; in which case you may stop where you choose, and sleep (like William Morris) with the sound of water a few inches from your ears.

One of the pioneers of this type of boat was Henry Taunt, the Oxford photographer, who in his *New Map of the River Thames* (first published in 1872) described his sleeping arrangements on board:

> My boat is what is termed in Oxford phrase, a Company boat, which is a broad gig with side-seats from the back rail, and an awning (which lets up and down); a locker for food was fitted behind the back rail. The boat is about 18ft long and 4ft 6in wide at the broadest part, and is fitted with the usual mast at the front seat; behind, close to the rudder-post, another short mast is fitted, which serves for a flag-staff during the day. When arranging for the night the awning is raised and fastened, then a side covering of good plain duck secured with strings all round to the iron which holds the awning, and fixed below the seat of the boat with loops, to buttons, thus completely enclosing the middle part of the boat. Between the side seats we place boards fitted on purpose . . . and the cushions on the top, with our carpet-bags at the head, to form the mattress . . . Thus we have a water-tight dry sleeping-place, and anything but an uncomfortable one.

The mast that Taunt mentions was a common feature of gigs and skiffs; a line could be attached to it for towing the boat, and sometimes a simple sail was hoist on it.

Taunt liked his food:

> I believe in a good beef-steak, cooked either over the coals or in the pan, when camping out; and this often formed the *pièce de résistance* of our dinner after a stiff day's work. Usually we had breakfast early, (just after our bathe—a thing which helps the appetite very much,) and made a good meal; in the middle of the day we feasted on crust and cheese, and washed it down with a

Henry Taunt and his camping gig by Wallingford Bridge, circa 1870.

glass of 'home-brew'd' kept for that purpose in a stone bottle; or, failing that, a glass of Thames water, qualified with whisky or some concentrated milk. When we reached our next camping-ground, (we usually moved each day,) we made our fire, and got dinner ready, taking tea with it; and a glass of 'the cratur', with a biscuit, sent us to bed at about nine o'clock at night.

### FARMOOR RESERVOIR AND ITS FISHERMEN

A mile downstream of Bablock Hythe the Thames makes a series of meanders, and then reaches Pinkhill Lock. On the right bank is the pumping station of the Farmoor Source Works, and behind it the huge reservoirs now controlled (like the river) by the Thames Water Authority. Water is pumped from the river and stored in the Stage One Reservoir, which covers 120 acres and can hold 1,000 million gallons. The water is then purified and piped away into the public supply. Farmoor is typical of water-works all along the Thames; their number is growing, and here a Stage Two Reservoir is being built to increase the yield. At the moment, no water may be drawn from the Thames at Farmoor if the river's flow past the pumping station falls to below

49

30 million gallons a day, as sometimes happens in a dry summer. When the Stage Two Reservoir is completed, it will actually put water *back into the river* in a dry season, and so help to supply water-works downstream.

Farmoor Reservoir is the home of a flourishing sailing club, and also of the Farmoor Fly Fishing Club. The fishing club has 300 members (and a waiting list of over 400); every year it stocks the reservoir with thousands of small brown and rainbow trout. This is one of the few places in the area where fly fishing for trout is possible, as the big Thames trout only pursue live bait and will not take a fly.

A founder member of the club was Fred Taylor, who was Secretary until his death in 1974. He kept a tackle shop in Oxford, was one of the best-known fishermen on the Thames, and fought many battles for the rights of anglers on the river. He and many other fishermen were, and are, concerned about the threat to the small local clubs who rent the fishing rights along short stretches of the river bank. Big syndicates from cities such as London, Birmingham and Coventry are putting in higher bids, and may eventually manage to exclude the local clubs almost entirely. One factor that has so far prevented this from happening is the size limit on the Thames; that is to say, fish caught that are below a certain size (the limit varies with the different species) must be put back into the water. The big syndicates prefer 'all-in' fishing, where any fish caught can be kept and allowed in a competition.

At Farmoor the fishermen and the sailing enthusiasts co-exist contentedly, sharing the water. On the Thames itself there are often less happy relations between the two groups. As motor cruisers get larger and more numerous, many fishermen are calling for restrictions on the size and number of the boats allowed on the river, before fishing is spoilt by congestion and the wash from the propellors.


EYNSHAM TO GODSTOW

Just below Pinkhill Lock is a boat hire station (the first since Lechlade) with a fleet of 'Carribean' cruisers, a type of boat of the size that many fishermen consider too big for the river. Certainly for good or ill they have become very popular, especially with families not used to boating holidays, who like the comfort of their roomy interiors. They are not, however, greatly loved by people in small boats who find themselves bobbing about in the wash made by these large vessels.

Now Swinford Toll Bridge comes into view, a handsome structure built in 1769 for the fourth Earl of Abingdon, whose descendants still receive the tolls charged for crossing the bridge. Before that date there was a ferry here, though it does not appear to have been very safe. In the winter of 1636 a party of Welsh sheriffs bringing ship money to Charles I were crossing when '3 or 4 were drown'd, £800 lost for a time, & 8 persons with some horses escaped by swimming', as Thomas Crosfield of Queen's College, Oxford, recorded at the time.

In 1764 John Wesley narrowly escaped disaster at Eynsham when riding from Oxford to visit friends at Witney. There seems at that time to have been a ford of some kind here as well (though how boats managed to get over it is not apparent). Wesley wrote in his journal:

> Between twelve and one we crossed Eynsham Ferry. The water was like a sea on both sides. I asked the ferryman, 'Can we ride the causeway?' He said, 'Yes, sir; if you keep in the middle.' But this was the difficulty, as the whole causeway was covered with water to a considerable depth; and this in many parts ran over the causeway with the swiftness and violence of a sluice. Once my mare lost both her fore feet, but she gave a spring, and recovered the causeway; otherwise we must have taken a swim, for the water on either side was ten or twelve feet deep. However, after one or two plunges more, we got through, and came safe to Witney.

In 1759 a curious old custom was recorded here. When the bounds of Cumnor parish on the Berkshire bank were beaten once a year, the ferryman at Swinford brought to the Vicar the sum of six shillings and eightpence in a bowl of water. The Vicar then crossed the river and took hold of the reeds on the Oxfordshire side, apparently laying claim to the whole breadth of the stream.

A little below Eynsham Lock a wharf stream leads away from the main channel on the north side; here within living memory barges came to take cargo to and from Eynsham village. This seems to have been the last place on the Thames above Oxford to have been served by barges. Rather over half a mile downstream, an old canal, generally called the Cassington Cut, runs into the Thames on the left-hand side; it was used by barges going to Cassington Mill. Now it is silted up and navigable only by canoes.

Canoeists are well served along this stretch of the river: the Evenlode, which enters the Thames shortly below Cassington Cut, offers them a chance to navigate as high as Charlbury; while the Seacourt Stream, which flows south from Hagley Pool a mile down river, provides good canoeing for many miles—and a way of avoiding Oxford and four locks, if you are in a light craft. Astonishingly, this little channel seems to have had a narrow escape from becoming the main navigation. In a House of Commons report of 1793 (a time when there was a passion for 'river improvements') a witness stated that 'the Navigation ought to have gone down the Witham Stream'. Fortunately it has remained a secluded backwater, running shallow past the

Ruins of Godstow Nunnery, photographed by Henry Taunt from the frozen river in 1895.

University Field Station and by the old mill house at Wytham. Then through Wytham village—where the White Hart Inn provides food and drink for weary canoeists—and alongside the Oxford eastern bypass road until the channel divides above Botley. Thence it is a pleasant paddle through the villages of North and South Hinksey (recalling Matthew Arnold's 'In the two Hinkseys nothing keeps the same') down to the railway line, the Abingdon road, and the main river, which is rejoined at Kennington railway bridge.

If you are travelling in a larger boat, the journey by the main stream has just as much to offer. Thames voyagers with time to spare, and a British Waterways Board licence, would do well to take their boats down Duke's Cut (which leaves the river via the Wolvercote mill stream just above King's Weir) and visit the Oxford Canal. It was opened to Oxford in 1790, and is one of the loveliest of inland waterways. Below Duke's Cut the side stream (not navigable now) leads to Wolvercote Paper Mill; paper has been made here for Oxford University and its Press since the early seventeenth century. John Aubrey the antiquarian wrote at the end of that century: 'At Wolvercot, ye right reverend Father in God, John Fell Lord Bishop of Oxford, caused white paper to be manufactured: and twas very good'. The

Floods on Port Meadow, circa 1868 (*Bodleian Library*).

mill gave up using water power in 1943; but the Thames still supplies thousands of gallons an hour for other parts of the paper-making process.

On the main stream of the river, Godstow comes next, with its ruined nunnery and legend of Fair Rosamund, of which Aubrey wrote (in a manuscript note inside his copy of Plot's *Natural History of Oxfordshire*, now in the Bodleian Library): 'This Rosamund, ye fair daughter of Walter Ld. Clifford, and forced to be Concubine to K. Henry ye 2d, who builded for her at Woodstock an house or Labyrinth under the ground, much wherof at this day is to be seen as also a goodly Bath or Well, called to this day Rosamund's Well. In the end she was poysoned by Q. Elianor, some write, and being dead, was buried at Godstow in a house of Nonnes besides Oxford. Not long since her grave was digged, where some of her bones were found, and her Teeth so white (as ye dwellers there report) that the beholders did much wonder at them.' Today Godstow Nunnery serves as a pound for beasts during the annual round-up held by the Sherriff of Oxford on Port Meadow.

### THE GOLDEN AFTERNOON

The towers and spires of Oxford are just visible across the broad expanse of Port Meadow. We are coming to the end of the Upper River, that strangely remote waterway which one old canal boatman used to call 'the West Country, by Bobluck Hoi'. Now we meet the sailing boats at Medley, and perhaps the occasional punt from Folly Bridge or even the Cherwell. It was along this reach that one of the most famous Oxford river-trips took place.

The Rev. Charles Lutwidge Dodgson was a lecturer in mathematics at Christ Church from 1855 until his death in 1898. Like many other bachelor Oxford dons of his day, one of his favourite pursuits on a summer's afternoon was to row on the river. By 1862 he had made the acquaintance of three daughters of Dean Liddell of Christ Church: Lorina, aged thirteen; Alice, aged ten; and Edith, aged eight. Seventy years later, Alice Liddell wrote in the *Cornhill Magazine*: 'When we went on the river for the afternoon with Mr Dodgson, which happened at most four or five times every summer term, he always brought out with him a large basket full of cakes, and a kettle, which we used to boil under a haycock, if we could find one . . . One of our favourite whole-day excursions was to row down to Nuneham to picnic in the woods there'.

Charles Dodgson's diary records for Tuesday 17 June 1862: 'Expedition to Nuneham. Duckworth (of Trinity) and Ina, Alice and Edith came with us . . . About a mile above Nuneham heavy rain came on, and after bearing it a short time I settled that we had better leave the boat and walk.' The next river trip was on Friday 4 July: 'Duckworth and I (wrote Dodgson) made an expedition *up* the river to Godstow with the three Liddells: we had tea on the bank there, and did not reach Christ Church again till quarter past eight, when we took them on to my rooms to see my collection of micro-photographs, and restored them to the Deanery just before nine.' On the opposite page Dodgson has written: 'On which occasion I told them the fairy-tale of *Alice's Adventures Underground*.' This was the story that was to be published three years later as *Alice's Adventures in Wonderland*, with the author disguising his identity behind the pseudonym 'Lewis Carroll'.

Dodgson later wrote (in *The Theatre*, 1887):

> Full many a year has slipped away since that 'golden after-noon' . . . but I can call it up almost as clearly as if it were yesterday—the cloudless blue above, the watery mirror below, the boat drifting idly on its way, the tinkle of the drops that fell from the oars, as they waved so sleepily to and fro, and (the one bright gleam of life in all the slumbrous scene) the three eager faces, hungry for news of fairy-land, and who would not be said 'nay' to—from whose lips 'Tell us a story, please' had all the stern immutability of Fate.

That was how Dodgson remembered the 'golden afternoon', though meteorological records actually indicate that the weather near Oxford on 4 July

1862, was 'cool and rather wet'.

The Rev. Robinson Duckworth of Trinity College accompanied the party, and recalled that he rowed stroke and Dodgson rowed bow, 'and the story was actually composed and spoken *over my shoulder* for the benefit of Alice Liddell, who was acting as "cox" of our gig.'

The episode of the Pool of Tears seems to have been inspired by the wetting Dodgson and the children had got on the earlier expedition to Nuneham. Otherwise the story (considering it was told on the Thames) seems to have derived surprisingly little of its inspiration from the river. But the verses which serve as a prologue to the book recall the occasion:

> All in the golden afternoon
> Full leisurely we glide;
> For both our oars, with little skill,
> By little arms are plied,
> While little hands make vain pretence
> Our wanderings to guide . . .
>
> Thus grew the tale of Wonderland:
> Thus slowly, one by one,
> Its quaint events were hammered out—
> And now the tale is done.
> And home we steer, a merry crew,
> Beneath the setting sun.

### TWO CENTURIES OF BOSSOMS

At Medley, near the foot of Port Meadow, the river divides into two streams. The left-hand channel leads to Medley Boat Station, while on the right stands Bossom's boatyard, where small craft of many kinds are built. There are no Bossoms connected with the firm now, but it preserves a name anciently associated with the Thames.

There were Bossoms on the Thames in the eighteenth century, if not earlier. *Jackson's Oxford Journal* records that in 1754 one Chas. Bossom, 'bargeman', was whipped for stealing ducks. In 1757 he was named as a ringleader of riots at Folly Bridge in Oxford, when corn was stolen from a wharf. In 1758 he was arrested in London and charged with stealing wheat, later he was acquitted. But in 1763 he was sentenced to be transported to America for seven years for a similar crime. He was still in America in 1772, perhaps by that time 'going straight'.

But the Bossom family continued to flourish on the Thames. In 1812 Thomas Bossom of Oxford had four barges trading on the river, including the

Narrow boat at Oxford, circa 1880 (*Henry Taunt*).

*Minner* of seventeen tons. In 1817 William Bossom was appointed keeper at Osney Lock, in 1822 James Bossom held Folly Bridge Lock, and in 1823 William Bossom was in charge at Medley Weir. He was succeeded by a John Bossom in 1838; Medley was again supervised by a William Bossom in 1854. From 1880 to 1894 C. Bossom was the ferryman at Gatehampton Ferry, Basildon; and in 1891 J. Bossom was keeper at King's Weir near Oxford, transferring to Clifton Hampden Lock in 1892. Besides working for the Thames Conservancy and its predecessors in these capacities, the Bossom family was also represented on the river by a business which undertook maintenance, pile driving and similar work. In the 1860s or 70s Squire Campbell of Buscot had three barges wedged in Osney Bridge: Charlie Bossom dislodged a boatload of stone to free them. And in 1878 when William Morris went up by boat from Medley to Kelmscott he had 'Bossom and another man to tow us as far as New Bridge.' Charlie Bossom died in 1911, and the business passed to his son. In 1935 he in turn handed it on to his son Tom Bossom, who retired in the 1960s and now lives near Abingdon.

Below Bossom's boatyard, on the right-hand channel, stood Medley Weir, the last of the Thames flash weirs (it was not removed until 1937). Among those who remember 'flashing' through it is Mr Fred Beauchamp, a retired canal boatman who lives in Oxford. He was a 'Number One' (a boatman who owned his own craft), and worked the *Phyllis*, a mule-drawn narrow boat which had belonged to his father. His regular working turn was along the Oxford Canal to and from the Midlands coalfields, but sometimes he would take *Phyllis* up to Eynsham to fetch 'ballast' or gravel from a dredger. He remembers that it was a difficult art to get the mule to pull the boat up through the weir almost as soon as it had been opened, before the water level dropped in the reach above.

Often Fred Beauchamp and *Phyllis* would bring coal from the Midlands down to the Oxford electricity company's generating station, which stands on the east bank of the Thames above Osney Lock. And occasionally *Phyllis* would go down the river as far as Wallingford with cargo on board. Mr Beauchamp remembers the Thames as 'different work altogether' from the canal, with a poor towpath in many places and a current which could make towing awkward. 'I didn't care much for the river,' he says, 'but if work was scarce, you had to take what you could get.'

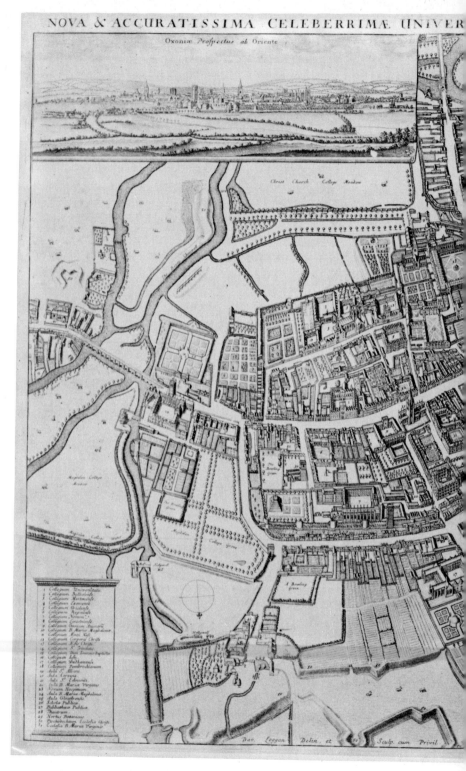

Map of Oxford in 1675 by David Loggan. The Castle Mill Stream of the Thames flows in from the north (bottom right-hand corner). At the first division of the river beyond the

Castle Mound,   the left-hand channel is the Trill Mill Stream.

# IV

# Oxford

The exact location of the ford from which Oxford takes its name is not known. It may have been where Folly Bridge now stands, on the important road to Abingdon and the south; or perhaps on the Cherwell at Magdalen Bridge, where the London road runs out of the town. Other fords existed over the streams crossed by the Botley road to the west of the city, and on the main river between Port Meadow and Binsey Green.

The Thames flows to the west and south of Oxford, and the Cherwell to the east, so that the city is three-quarters surrounded by water; its environs must in ancient times have been virtually a marsh, a good defence against invaders. A number of courses are taken by the Thames through the town and the surrounding area, some of them natural, some artificial. The Oxford chronicler Anthony à Wood, writing in 1661, called them 'so many veines that spread from the greater, which make severall little isles wherein our praedicessors have erected religious aedifices'.

There were indeed a number of important monasteries and convents in mediæval Oxford, many of which were (as Wood puts it) 'encompassed with pleasant waters to the great delight of the monasticks that lived in them.' Many of these religious houses owned mills, and so had a vested interest in a stream that passed their cloisters. If there were no convenient stream, they diverted one: the modern navigation channel between Four Streams (the junction with the Oxford Canal by the railway station) and the confluence with the Pot Stream below Osney Lock is thought to be an artificial 'cut' dug for the monks of Osney Abbey, to supply their mill with water.

At Osney Lock the Thames Water Authority has its maintenance yard and navigation office, serving the district from Cricklade to Wallingford Bridge. From this point to Folly Bridge the river passes through rather bleak surroundings, railway bridges, car parks, building sites and the remains of gasworks, all something of a disappointment for the river traveller

Abel Beesley, Oxford Waterman and champion punter, circa 1910 (*Henry Taunt*).

who expects a prospect of an ancient university city. A bargeman of several centuries ago would have found himself steering his boat much closer to the heart of Oxford, for in those days vessels coming down the river from Godstow would probably have taken the eastern channel at Medley and come down it to Hythe Bridge (or High Bridge as it was sometimes called), where there was a busy wharf. A short distance below, by Quaking Bridge, was the Castle Mill which stood under the shadow of Oxford Castle until 1929. Boats could not pass it, but apparently they could navigate the stream which runs slightly to the west of Hythe Bridge and under Bookbinders' Bridge. According to a mediæval plan of the castle there seems to have been a flash weir on this channel. By this route boats would eventually rejoin the present navigation a little above Folly Bridge.

The Hythe Bridge wharf was busy until the early years of this century, when it was still being used by narrow boats from the Oxford Canal (although the canal also had its own wharf at the terminal basin where Nuffield College now stands). Fisher Row by Hythe Bridge housed many boatmen's families. Among those doing business there was Abel Beesley, a waterman famed as a champion punter. In 1910 he challenged a steam launch to race his punt between Medley and Godstow, and won by 110 yards!

The tunnel which carries the Trill Mill Stream under Oxford.

### THE TRILL MILL STREAM

Near Oxford Castle an iron sluice guards the mouth of a tunnel about four feet wide and of the same height. This is the western entrance to the Trill Mill Stream, which leaves the Castle Mill Stream (as the Thames is called here) opposite Paradise Street. It flows under the car parks of St Ebbe's, along Rose Place, and beneath St Aldate's, to emerge in the Christ Church Memorial Garden. Thence it continues (open to view) past Linacre House and the police station, to rejoin the main river just below Folly Bridge. This mainly underground watercourse, known by many and journeyed down by few, is part of Oxford folklore.

The Trill Mill Stream is thought to be artificial in origin, and may have been dug by the Saxons. In mediæval times it was up to a hundred feet wide in places, and may even have carried the greater part of the Thames through Oxford (as seems likely from recent archaeological investigations). It turned at least five mills, one of which was owned by the Dominicans or Black Friars, who built Preacher's Bridge over the stream, a name commemorated by the modern Preacher's Pool above Folly Bridge. The Trill Mill itself stood where the Christ Church Memorial Garden has now been laid out. (It is probably no coincidence that an old mill-stone lies on the meadow path just beyond this garden.) A number of other watercourses flowed into and out of the Trill, among them the Shirelake, which formed the boundary between Oxfordshire and Berkshire.

The Trill and its associated streams formed an integral part of mediæval Oxford south of the city wall. It was an important supply of fresh water; but it was also a convenient drain or even a common sewer. Bakers, brewers and laundresses used it; so did tanners, and probably butchers too; and worst of all, the local 'houses of easement' emptied filth into it. In 1293 Edward I ordered that the 'corrupt water of Trillmill stream' should not be used in making bread or ale; but in the seventeenth century the situation was just as bad, and Anthony à Wood complained of the 'very unwholesome liquor' brewed from its waters. When John Taylor, the 'Water Poet', wrote in 1644 of the contamination of the Thames in Oxford, he was probably thinking of the Trill Mill Stream:

> Dead Hogges, Dogges, Cats, and well flayd Carryon Horses,
> Their noysom Corpes sould the Water Courses:
> Both swines and Stable dunge, Beasts guts and Garbage,
> Street durt, with Gardners weeds and Rotten Herbage.
> And from those Waters filthy putrifaction,
> Our meat and drinke were made, which bred Infection.

Even as late as the nineteenth century the Trill Mill Stream seems to have contributed to disease. There were cholera epidemics in 'the Friars', the area of working-class houses bordered by the stream, where once the Black Friars had their monastery, and after the second of these epidemics, in 1854, the stream was culverted and covered over in many places. Now it is subterranean for most of its length, a challenge for adventurous canoeists.

A first hand account of navigating it was given by two undergraduates, Jonathan Bailey and Roger Robinson, in a letter to the *Oxford Mail* in 1958: 'The stream was very low for our expedition. We ran aground three times, and holed the canvas of our canoe, to which we had to effect a temporary repair by torchlight before going on. The whole voyage made against the stream from Christ Church to the Castle, took us half-an-hour.'

Recently the Trill Mill Stream was diverted through two right-angle bends so that a new multi-storey car park could be built, and it is now even more difficult to navigate. Anyone wanting to try should contact the Oxford City Engineer's department, which looks after the stream and controls the water level.

As it flows under Rose Place, the Trill Mill Stream passes the University Catholic Chaplaincy. Ronald Knox, Catholic Chaplain for many years, was fascinated by this underground watercourse outside his front door, and when in 1952 he published a book of sermons or 'conferences', he called it *The Hidden Stream*, and drew from the title this moral: 'Not all the philosophies of Oxford are philosophies of negation and despair; she is fed by secret streams, not less influential to her life or less native to her genius.'

63

Folly Bridge.

## FOLLY BRIDGE AND SALTER'S STEAMERS

Folly Bridge was originally called South Bridge or Grand Pont. A bridge is supposed to have been built here in 1085 by Robert d'Oilli, a powerful Norman who (according to legend) molested the local religious houses, and in particular deprived Abingdon Abbey of an important piece of land. The Abingdon monks prayed to the Virgin Mary for help. One night d'Oilli dreamt that he saw the Virgin in a vision, and that she sent him out into a meadow, where he was tormented by ruffians who 'pissed fire upon him' and 'cinged and burnt his beard'. He awoke in terror, repented of his misdeeds, and built Folly Bridge as a penance. (According to some sources his benefaction was actually Hythe Bridge.)

A curious building called Friar Bacon's Study formerly stood across the north end of Folly Bridge, and was apparently responsible for the name 'Folly'. Roger Bacon, a Franciscan Friar of Oxford who died in 1292, used it as an observatory, and was thought by the common people to be a necromancer. The Study was demolished in 1779. Today a castellated house by the bridge bears the name 'The Folly'.

The old Folly Bridge lay at an awkward angle to the stream and presented a great obstacle to boats. Robert Burton of Christ Church is said to have amused himself in the intervals of writing his *Anatomy of Melancholy* (published in 1621) by coming down here to watch the bargemen in difficulties and listen to their curses. From 1821 till 1884 a pound lock stood across

*Alaska*, the first Salter's steamer *(Salter Bros)*.

the channel which runs to the south of the main bridge, where there was a fall in summer of one and a half to two feet. The channel is now open and unobstructed.

Folly Bridge is the home of Salter's, one of the oldest and best-known firms of Thames boatbuilders and pleasure craft operators. It was established in 1858 by John and Stephen Salter and Isaac King, who built small pleasure craft, and John Salter's sons soon came into the business. In 1888 the firm introduced its first passenger service, with its steam launch *Alaska* making a weekly trip between Oxford and Kingston. *Alaska* was in service for many decades, and at the time of writing her wooden hull is still intact and likely to be restored.

This was not the first regular passenger steamer service in the locality, as the Thames & Isis Steamboat Co. of Abingdon was already operating two passenger boats, the steam launches *Thames* and *Isis*. But Salter's soon became a leading operator of passenger trips. In 1889 their next boat was delivered, a steel-hulled twin-screw steamer named *Oxford* and built by Clark's of Brimscombe (on the Thames & Severn Canal). In the succeeding years Clark's built more boats for Salters: *Kingston, Cliveden, Windsor* and *Henley*. In 1898 Salters themselves built *Nuneham*, which was soon followed by *Marlow* and *Sonning*. In the following years came *Streatley, Goring* and *Wargrave*. Today these names can still be seen in the Salter's fleet, though the boats in use at the present time were built at a later date.

By the early 1900s Salter's steamers were calling twice daily at all the places between Oxford and Kingston. Meanwhile Salter's were building all types of craft at Folly Bridge: passenger steamers up to 105 feet long, college barges, houseboats, skiffs, punts, canoes, and (in later years) motor cabin cruisers. The firm was especially well known for its 'camping boats', the covered skiffs and punts which were delivered and collected by Salters to and from any point on the Thames.

Salter's passenger launches no longer make the continuous two and a half day trip from Oxford to Kingston, as the service was curtailed at the end of 1973 for economic reasons. But a regular passenger timetable still operates between Oxford and Abingdon, Wallingford and Reading, Reading and Henley, Marlow and Windsor, and Windsor and Walton. Combined rail and river tickets are still available for a day's outing from London, and the Salter's boats may still be hired for private parties. The last true steamers in the fleet ceased operating in the 1960s, and the firm's passenger launches are now diesel powered.

Today boat building continues at Salters but now most of their time is spent making glass fibre dinghies, punts and motor boats as well as wooden racing shells.

AN OXFORD WATERMAN

Below Folly Bridge is the finishing point of Oxford University's rowing course, which starts just above Iffley Lock. The two principal sets of races in the University year are Torpids, in the Easter Term, and Summer Eights, which take place at the end of May and beginning of June.

Christ Church Meadow spreads itself along the north bank of the course, and a short way downstream are the two mouths of the Cherwell, the lower of which is the artificial 'New Cut'. The Cherwell is navigable by light un-powered craft, and is chiefly used by punts, which can be hired at Magdalen Bridge, and at a boathouse further upstream in North Oxford (or from Folly Bridge on the Thames itself). Punts can get up the Cherwell as far as Islip, and canoes can navigate many miles beyond that.

Along the Christ Church bank of the Thames there used to be moored twenty-two magnificent ceremonial barges, each belonging to one of the men's colleges in the University. They were used to provide changing-rooms for the crews and a tea-room and grandstand for members of the colleges and their families. Now the barges are almost all gone from here (though a few are being restored nearby), and their place has been taken by a row of modern boathouses, most of which are shared by a pair of colleges.

The first boat-races at Oxford were held in the early nineteenth century.

An Edwardian Eights Week, in the heyday of both college barge and small boat (*Henry Taunt*).

At that time it was the custom for sporting undergraduates to row to the King's Arms Inn at Sandford Lock, take supper, and row back. These jaunts became a regular affair, and the men took to using eight-oared boats and racing each other home. The boats would gather in Iffley Lock, which could accommodate four 'eights'. When the gates opened, each crew would push its boat out in turn, and so the race would start in single file with each boat trying to catch the one in front and bump it. These bumping races soon became an organised event; meanwhile boat-racing in eights also became fashionable at Cambridge, and in 1829 the first Oxford and Cambridge Boat Race was rowed at Henley. It was won by Oxford.

The first 'eights' were massive clinker-built boats with no outriggers, and they looked rather like ships' lifeboats. The racing eight as we know it only began to appear towards the end of the nineteenth century; sliding seats were a late development, the earliest method of giving the oarsman mobility being to smear his seat with grease.

In the clubrooms above the college boathouses there are rows of names in gold lettering on wood, recording, as each crew quickly supersedes the last, the fleeting successes of Oxford rowing men. But for generations of them, a constant factor has been the face of their waterman. There are now twelve watermen serving the rowing clubs of the University, eleven of them working for the colleges. Nearly all of them come of old-established riverside families, and several are related to one another.

One of them, Albert Andrews, serves no individual college but is Waterman

Method of starting a college boat at Iffley Lock before 1825.

to the Oxford University Boat Club, the club that exists primarily to row against Cambridge in the annual Boat Race. He, too, comes of a family of boatmen, and has three brothers still working as watermen at Oxford. Unlike the college boatmen he lives on the job. His home is at the back of the Oxford University Boathouse, a building that stands alone on its side of the river, grander and more in keeping with the traditions of Oxford rowing than the modern college boathouses on the opposite bank. But the O.U.B.C. built its boathouse on land leased from University College. The lease reverted some years ago, and the club then lost its clubroom and half its boathouse to the landlord.

Like all the Oxford watermen, Albert Andrews' work is many-sided; he has to be by turns boatbuilder and repairer, steersman, organiser of events and rowing coach, his tasks changing with the calendar of the rowing year.

Before the beginning of the Michaelmas term at the University he must have repaired and revarnished all the boats in his care, ready for a winter of selection and training for the Boat Race which, though some six months ahead, is always in view. When term starts in October, each man with a hope of selection is tried out in a rowing eight or a smaller boat, and the numbers are whittled down to just four eights, who then undergo trials at the end of term.

The Thames at Oxford is nothing like the broad tidal Thames at London, where the race is rowed. So before long the prospective crew must train either on the Boat Race course itself or on something approximating to it. They will

Thomas Timms, University Waterman, with starting gun for a race, at Iffiley, circa 1900 (*Henry Taunt*).

Albert Andrews, University Waterman, at Henley Royal Regatta, 1974.

probably practise at Henley at the end of the Michaelmas term, and then, after Christmas, train on the tideway itself for two weeks. The beginning of the Easter term means that the crews have to be back in residence in their colleges, so training has to continue in local waters. A good substitute for the tideway is Wallingford, where there are six miles of lock-free river. The waterman, coaches and crew have a private system of landmarks there, each representing a feature of the Boat Race course (the milepost, Hammersmith Bridge, Chiswick Steps, and the rest).

Two weeks before the Boat Race, training begins again on the tideway at Putney. The Cambridge crew usually arrives at the same time, and uses a boathouse that is nearly next door, but the rivalry is generally friendly.

On the day of the race itself, Albert Andrews has to check every nut, bolt and thumbscrew on the boat. The crew has a short outing, and then the boat is polished and guarded until the race, against the many people who would 'just like to touch'. The time of the start is dictated by the tide; Albert Andrews is there to put the crew into the boat and give his final words of encouragement.

In all his years as waterman he has only seen the race from beginning to end three times; usually his job makes it impossible. He watches the crew for the first stretch in case something stops the race (one year, for instance, Oxford's rudder-lines broke shortly after the start, and had to be repaired immediately). With the crew safely out of sight, he goes by road to Mortlake, where he meets the boat after the finish. When the race is over, he has one remaining task: packing the boat back on its trailer, ready for the return journey to Oxford.

The Boat Race is the culmination of all the Oxford University Boat Club's efforts, but is only the beginning of a season of rowing events in which the club takes part, and Albert Andrews now prepares for a summer of organising stakeboats, starters, cannon and ferries. After Eights Week at Oxford, the regatta season begins, usually at Reading; and by the time Marlow, Henley, Staines and Maidenhead Regattas have come and gone, the waterman's year has come full circle.


### VICTORIANA RESTORED

Not far below the O.U.B.C. boathouse, the modern Donnington Bridge spans the river. In a backwater just above it, you can usually see one or two of the old College barges being restored by the Oxford College Barge Preservation Trust.

The tradition of ornamental barges at Oxford began with six London Guild barges brought to the city in the middle of the nineteenth century.

St John's College barge under restoration at Donnington Bridge.

More were built to order, until eventually there were twenty-two, each rivalling the next in splendour of decoration and accommodation for spectators. But the barges were built of timber, and the life-expectancy of a timber hull is perhaps one hundred years. One by one they became unsafe and had to be towed away, many to remain on the Thames down-river as houseboats, some to be broken up. The barges were nearly all gone from Oxford when in 1966 a few enthusiastic people founded the Preservation Trust to restore and care for a number of the surviving specimens.

Between 1967 and 1969 the Jesus College barge was completely restored and given a new teak hull; this was done at the personal expense of the High Sheriff of Maidenhead, and at present the barge is moored in that town. The Hertford College barge had been partially restored when it was damaged by fire, and it is now being repaired at a Teddington boatyard. The Corpus Christi and St John's barges are being restored at Donnington Bridge, but work is of necessity slow and expensive.

The restoration is organised by the Trust's technical adviser, Mr Robert Maccoun (an American by birth). He hopes that eventually five or six barges will be fully restored and returned to their original moorings, where they would form the basis of a museum of rowing and the Thames.

HARRIS AND SON

A little downstream of Donnington Bridge, on the way to Iffley Lock, the

David Harris at work on a racing boat.

towpath passes a modest two-storey boathouse, the upper floor of which is the main workshop of George Harris & Son, boatbuilders.

It is a small firm, typical of many to be found on the Thames between Oxford and London. Of the staff of five, three are members of the Harris family, but only one, David, works at boat-building full-time. His father, George Harris, is the Christ Church waterman, and during the University term spends only his mornings with the firm. His cousin Len is boatman to another college, and does the same. Tom Rose, son of the landlord of the neighbouring Isis Hotel, and Steve Gaisford, who came to Harris's from Salter's, make up the five. Harris's have orders for racing boats from all over the world. They can build a racing eight in about four weeks, at a price not much more than half that charged by Continental boatbuilders.

The business began in the 1880s when George Harris's father (also named George) began building skiffs and punts in his back garden. It was the height of the small pleasure-craft's popularity, and business expanded. Harris took over a boat hire station at Folly Bridge (opposite Salter's) and even ran a pleasure steamer from Oxford to Abingdon. There was no room for boat-building at Folly Bridge, so for many years the boats were built at premises near the Oxford gasworks. The firm moved to the present site because it was cleaner.

George Harris was, as a boy, more interested in rowing than in the pleasure boat trade, and so at the age of seventeen he began working for the Christ Church boat club, and has coached, and maintained boats, for the college ever since. He became a champion-class sculler, but as a waterman he was debarred from all the big amateur rowing events including Henley Regatta.

Like others who found themselves on the wrong side of it, George Harris is still bitter about the wall that divided 'professionals' from 'gentleman amateurs' in pre-war rowing. The watermen had their own clubs and events (he himself rowed for Oxford Watermen), but there was still the rub that because they could be paid for coaching or might have a cash stake on a race they were said by the amateurs to 'row for gain'. George Harris is vehement that none of the 'professionals' he knew ever rowed for anything but the sport of it.

The rules of the major rowing events have since been eased, but to have been paid for coaching still disqualifies for life. In this context it is a distinction of which George Harris is wryly proud that he was invited in 1973 to be a member of the panel of coaches for the Oxford University crew—the first 'professional' ever to join the ranks of the Old Blues.

The boat business at Folly Bridge passed to George Harris from his father in 1947. In turn, George's son David left school for boatbuilding, and was apprenticed at Timm's Oxford boatyard, specialising in the building of racing boats. At the same time the skiff and punt hire business was declining with the growing popularity of motor cruisers, so when David Harris finished his apprenticeship in 1960 his father decided to give up hiring boats. George Harris & Son have specialised in building racing boats ever since, and the firm has flourished.

Fashions in racing boats change constantly. Every customer tends to want a boat like the one that won the last important race, and over the last few years there has been a notable influx of foreign (especially Italian) ideas in boatbuilding. In materials, too, there have been considerable developments. Fifty years ago the 'skin' of a racing boat was of solid cedar, which had to be steamed from end to end, the most difficult and time-consuming of tasks. Cedar is hard to come by today, and it has in any case been replaced in boatbuilding by plywood, used so thin that it has the lightness of cedar, while being stronger and far easier to mould. Harris's now use the Italian 'cold moulding' process, and steam only the tightest of bends. 'Skinning', the strapping, glueing and nailing of the flat shape on to the curved frame of the boat, is nevertheless still the hardest part of the craft.

Harris's make every wooden part of the boat; non-wood fittings come to them from other firms. A racing eight of the simplest design ordered from

Coach and six on the frozen river at Christ Church Meadows, February 1895 (*Henry Taunt*).

them in 1974 would have cost the customer a little over a thousand pounds excluding tax. But few customers today want simple boats, and the extras, such as shoes, or a boat made in sections for easy transporting, can add up to nearly double the price.

At lunch time, George and David Harris walk the few hundred yards up the towpath to the family house at Long Bridges. Although few people are fortunate enough to live so near their place of work, the towpath here is an important thoroughfare for walkers and cyclists going from South Oxford to the centre of the city. One college waterman even comes to work by boat from his home near Osney Lock. But scarcely anybody can have such a short distance to go as Tom Rose, who when he finishes work at Harris's goes next door to the Isis Hotel where his father Bill is landlord. Bill Rose is dependent on the river; during his many years at the pub he has fetched his own beer by water. The Isis is not accessible by road, so the barrels and crates are loaded on to a punt at Donnington Bridge and poled down to the pub.

# V

# Messing About in Boats: Iffley to Reading

In the stonework just below Iffley Lock an ornamental mooring ring marks the start of the Oxford rowing course. From the lock it is little more than a mile downstream before the roaring of weirs can be heard again, and soon the chimney of Sandford paper mill marks Sandford Lock, recently enlarged and now one of the biggest on this stretch of river. The sandy bed of the river here suggests the origin of the place name.

The fall at Sandford is considerable, and was increased artificially many years ago to give the mill a good head of water. So the main weir falls with great force into the pool below, which is known as Sandford Lasher, and has long been notorious for drownings. A stone obelisk stands in the middle of the weir, and on its base are the names of Richard Phillimore and William Gaisford who were drowned here in 1843, and of George Dasent, drowned in 1872. All three were Christ Church men, and they were not the only members of that college to lose their lives here.

On Thursday 19 May 1921, J. M. Barrie, author of *Peter Pan* and many other successful plays, was at his flat at the Adelphi in London. He was in his sixty-second year, and had just had a short holiday in Dorset with one of his wards, Michael Llewellyn Davies. Sir James Barrie had become guardian to the Llewellyn Davies boys after the death of their parents, and they were his closest friends; he called them 'my boys'. The *Peter Pan* story had been invented to amuse them. And Michael, nearly twenty-one, was Barrie's special favourite. He was an undergraduate at Christ Church, and had just gone back to college.

On the Thursday evening Barrie wrote a letter to Michael, as he did every day when they were apart, and took it down with him in the lift to post it. In the hall he was met by a newspaper reporter with the news that Michael had been drowned in Sandford Lasher. He and his friend Rupert Buxton had been bathing there; Michael could hardly swim at all, and had a fear of water. He had found himself out of his depth and got into difficulties. His

Sandford Lasher.

friend (it was believed) tried to save him and was dragged down. A man from the paper mill saw what was happening and threw in a life-belt, but it was too late.

Michael's death was a blow from which Barrie never entirely recovered. Perhaps it was he who arranged for another inscription to be carved on the memorial stone which had already stood above the weir pool for nearly eighty years:

Michael Llewelyn Davies
and
Rupert Erroll Victor Buxton
commoners of Christ Church
were drowned here on the
19th May 1921.

## NUNEHAM

Below Sandford a long reach without landmarks leads to the modern boat-house which belongs to Radley College, a public school with a strong rowing tradition. On the opposite bank the mansion of Nuneham Park peeps occasionally through the trees, though for the most part it keeps well hidden. It was built for the first Earl Harcourt in 1756, but after he had lost his life by falling down a well in the grounds in 1777, the original Palladian mansion

The Thames at Nuneham, 1811. The bridge to the island remained until recently.

and park were remodelled for the second Earl by Capability Brown. The house and grounds belong to Oxford University and are now used by a teacher training college, and so are only open to the public occasionally. The wood at the foot of Nuneham Park which forms the river frontage is known as 'Lock Wood' from the flash weir that stood here until the mid-nineteenth century (flash weirs being often referred to as 'locks').

The business of walking along the towpath becomes hazardous below Oxford, for the path changes frequently from side to side, chiefly because of the attitude of riparian owners in past centuries. Until recent years this did not matter very much, as there was always a ferry at places where the path crossed sides. Up to the Second World War the Thames Conservancy was maintaining nineteen such ferries, but in 1953 it was decided that they should cease operation. Nowadays there is no provision for crossing at these points, and a wide detour is often necessary before the path can be regained. This happens just above Abingdon lock, and you will have to walk through Abingdon before you can cross the river and get back to the towpath. There *is* a convenient railway bridge at Nuneham, but iron notices erected many years ago by the Great Western Railway warn you against crossing that way, so this is not a course that can be openly recommended.

A stream separates from the Thames a mile below Nuneham on the left-hand side going down-river. But this is no mere back-water (as modern maps sometimes designate it), for it has a claim to be the main river itself, and goes under the ancient title of the Swift Ditch.

There is evidence to suggest that before the tenth century the greater part of the Thames flowed down the Swift Ditch, even that it was the sole course of the river between Nuneham and Culham. The present navigation through Abingdon is apparently at least in part a 'cut' which was dug in the tenth century for the monks of Abingdon Abbey, much as the Osney monks in Oxford dug a channel for their use. It cannot, however, have been entirely artificial, as some kind of natural channel must have existed to bring the waters of the River Ock into the Thames.

For many centuries the navigation took this newer stream through Abingdon and avoided the Swift Ditch. But by the early 1600s there was trouble from shallows or 'shoals' in it, and in 1632 John Taylor wrote:

> At *Abington* the shoales are worse and worse,
> That *Swift ditch* seems to be the better course.

His opinion was shared by the Oxford-Burcot Commissioners, a body closely concerned with this part of the river. Indeed they were the first body of any kind to have official control over the river, albeit only a section of it, and this seems a good point to turn aside and briefly consider the events that led up to their formation.

Until the seventeenth century the Thames was almost a law unto itself. The first significant charter connected with the river was given by Richard I to the City of London in 1197, and commanded that 'all weirs within the Thames be removed, wheresoever they shall be . . .' On this document rested the authority which the City of London often claimed in later centuries over the whole river.

Weirs were certainly troublesome, for though they assisted the navigation by providing good floating depth, they were also a lucrative source of tolls. Weirs also caused floods, and were responsible for the wholesale destruction of fish, which was often taken away by the cartload, sometimes merely for pig food or manure. So it was that the twenty-third clause of Magna Carta, signed alongside the Thames at Runnymede in 1215, decreed that 'all weirs from henceforth shall be utterly put down by Thames and Medway, and the whole of England, except only by the sea coast'. (The Latin word actually used in the charter is *kidelli* which probably means specifically 'fishing weirs'.)

But despite Magna Carta and many later pieces of legislation, the weirs remained and indeed proliferated, with the result that navigation was a slow and extremely expensive business. Meanwhile barges became bigger and more numerous, and in the sixteenth century it must have been a common sight to see them stranded on the shallows in a dry summer, while their crews argued with the miller at the next weir upstream, trying to persuade him to let more water through.

By 1600 complaints about the navigation had become centred upon the part of the river between Oxford and Burcot, a village a little below Clifton Hampden. Barges could not get above Burcot because of shallow water, and had to be unloaded there, and their cargo taken on to Oxford by road. It was expensive and tiresome, especially as many of the barges were bringing stone and timber for the expanding University. So in 1605 James I signed an Act appointing eighteen Commissioners to have powers 'for the clearing effecting or perfecting' of the Thames between Burcot and Oxford.

The Commissioners were representatives of the University and City of Oxford, but although they held a meeting and apparently surveyed the river in 1607, nothing else was done, and in 1611 Sir Thomas Bodley managed to acquire some timber for enlarging his library at Oxford, 'which timber was to have been employed for making the Thames navigable to Oxford, but that work does not proceed'. By 1620 the state of the river prompted the University to get another Act passed 'for the making of the Ryver of Thames navygable from Byrcott to Oxford', and this time eight Commissioners were appointed. The great difference from the earlier Act was that this one empowered them 'to make and erect any Wharfes Lockes or Turnepickes or Pennes for Water . . . that shalbe fitt or necessarie'. The word 'turnepicke' referred to a device that was by no means new, but had not yet been used on the Thames: the pound lock, with top and bottom gates for 'impounding' the water, and sluices for lowering and raising it. This Act was responsible for the building of the first such locks on the river.

### THE FIRST POUND-LOCKS

Who exactly invented the pound lock will probably always be something of a mystery. The Ancient Egyptians are believed to have had some system of gates on their canal which linked the Mediterranean and the Red Sea, and the Chinese have also been credited with the invention, though according to one traveller they had only smooth stone banks up which boats had to be hauled to reach the higher level. Probably the birthplace of the pound lock was that source of so many inventions, Renaissance Italy, for Leo Battista Alberti writing in 1452 described what is recognizably the modern type of lock, with 'two stops, cutting the river in two places, and leaving a space between them equal to the length of a vessel'.

It may be that the first pound locks actually constructed were by Philippe

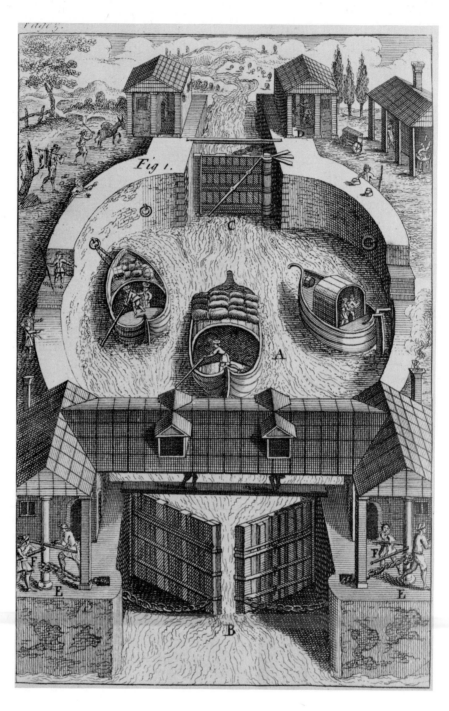

A Dutch lock in the seventeenth century, from John Ray's *Travels through the Low Countries*.

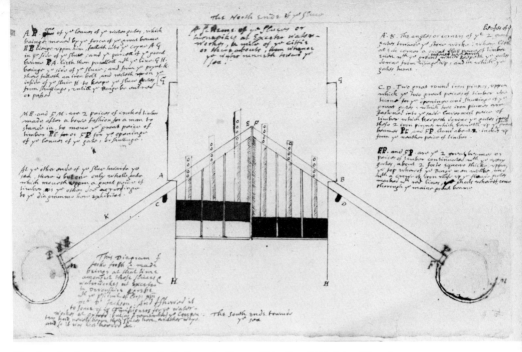

The drawing by Brian Twyne of a lock on the Exeter Ship Canal (*Bodleian Library*).

Marie Visconti some time around 1440. Later, in about 1475, pound locks were built on the Milanese canal, a navigational project which involved, as did many others, the engineering facet of Leonardo da Vinci's genius. In the *Codex Atlantico* collection of his drawings there is a page of lock designs: on the left of the page is a guillotine type gate which was raised first by chains being wound round a pole above it, and then see-sawed above the lock by leaning on the protruding end of the pole. This simple type of gate was soon superseded by the pair of 'mitred' gates, joining at an angle so that the pressure of water against them helps to keep them shut. Leonardo is believed to have been himself responsible for this sophistication. (Among his drawings are also designs for a dredging-boat and a life-jacket, both very close to those in use at the present day.)

The idea of the pound lock seems to have travelled quickly from Italy to France, and to Holland. An illustration from John Ray's *Travels through the Low Countries*, published in 1673, shows the design of a Dutch lock. It is oval, and contains three boats with room to spare; at its top end is a mitred pair of gates, but at the bottom only a single gate; to open it, each gate has, attached to its unhinged end, a chain which can be hauled in round a capstan. The whole of the lock-keeper's area of work is roofed in, and the lock seems excellently organized. It was probably a Dutch model like this that was copied when the first pound lock was built in Britain.

This was on the Exeter Ship Canal, built in 1563 so that ships could come up to Exeter without using the River Exe, which like the Thames was

Swift Ditch Lock.

obstructed by weirs designed to bring in profit to the landowners. The canal was designed by an engineer called John Trew, of Glamorgan, and it had three pound locks of essentially the same design as those used in Holland, except that instead of being oval they were straight-sided. They were probably built of wood; certainly that was the case when a lock was built in the Lea at Waltham in the 1570s.

The Oxford-Burcot Commissioners decided to build three pound locks or 'turnepickes' on the fourteen mile stretch of water that they were required to improve. One was at Iffley, the second at Sandford, and these two were built alongside existing weirs and were finished by 1638, if not earlier. But which course was the navigation to take below Nuneham? Was it to go along the Abingdon channel, or down the Swift Ditch which John Taylor had thought 'the better course'? The question seems to have been undecided as late as 1639, for in the summer of that year the Oxford University Archivist Brian Twyne recorded that the Commissioners were meeting at Abingdon to discuss 'y$^e$ old passage of y$^e$ Barges to Oxford, and whether it were through Swift Ditch or no'. Presumably they had decided to adopt which ever was the 'old passage' or original course of the Thames, and when this was agreed to be Swift Ditch they decided that it should once again become the navigation channel. The third lock was then built in Swift Ditch at a point shortly after that stream leaves the main river, and the remains of that lock can still be seen there today.

Where did the Oxford-Burcot Commissioners get their lock designs?

Certainly Brian Twyne had been to Exeter, for he made a drawing of one of John Trew's locks and showed it to the Commissioners when he got back to Oxford; it is thought to be the earliest surviving drawing of an English lock, and is now in the Bodleian Library. Besides the gates and sluices Twyne recorded an 'iron bolt to keep y^e gates open' and the two-foot square beams 'upon y^e top whereof y^e Bargemen walke & with a crown of iron raise up y^e floude gates'. But Twyne's drawing had come too late, for 'y^e carpenters had newely begun their sluices here another waye and so it was not heeded'. It is impossible to say what the 'other way' was; perhaps the number of arrangement of sluices was different, or perhaps it was simply the fact that the new locks were to have mitred pairs of gates at both ends, not just upstream.

And so the Oxford-Burcot Commissioners could pride themselves that they had built the first locks on the Thames, locks which were no doubt admired by all who came to see them. Dr Plot wrote in his *Natural History of Oxfordshire* (1677) describing them as 'a great pair of Folding doors, or Flood-gates of Timber cross the River . . . Within these there is a large square taken out of the river, built up at each side with Free-Stone, big enough to receive the largest barge afloat.' The new locks, however, do not seem to have been enough to make the river navigable at all times of the year, for in the same book Plot records that 'in dry times, barges do sometimes lie aground three weeks, or a month, or more;' and in 1685 Anthony à Wood recorded that because of the dry summer 'the boatmen can not goe from Oxon to London but take boats at Bircot.'

The barges (when the water was high enough) went on using the route via Swift Ditch and its lock until 1790. In this year several 'gentlemen of Abingdon', no doubt keen for financial reasons to get the boat traffic back to their town, initiated the building of Abingdon Lock on its present site on the northern channel, and Swift Ditch fell out of use almost at once. The Swift Ditch Lock was therefore abandoned, and in 1802 Robert Mylne, conducting a survey for the Thames Commissioners (a later body not to be confused with the Oxford-Burcot Commissioners) found it 'all deserted and ruinous'. But he added: 'The stonework, though long left to itself, is still sound, and better than the modern work.' The 'modern work' he referred to was the type of lock built in the 1780s, chiefly of timber, and without the good quality stonework of the earlier constructions.

Swift Ditch Lock was built so well that it would be useable today had not its gates long since rotted away. It lies a little way along the eastern channel of the Ditch, just below the outfall from the navigation. The Ditch itself can now only be navigated by canoes, but it is well worth exploring. Half way down is a quiet pool where once the barges tied up before ascending a weir; at the tail it flows under a handsome bridge built in 1416 in the tradition of Radcot and Newbridge; below this it rejoins the main river.

Abingdon Bridge was built in the same year as the bridge over the Swift Ditch at Culham. Leland records of its construction: 'Every man had a Penny a Day, which was the best Wages, and an Extraordinary Price in those times.' In the 1920s it had its central arches knocked out as part of an 'improvement' scheme, and they were replaced by a broad span which allows boats to pass through easily, but is out of keeping with the rest of the bridge. Note the fine wharf in Abingdon near St Helen's Church, and also the handsome iron bridge over the mouth of the Ock, built by the proprietors of the now derelict Wilts & Berks Canal, which entered the Thames nearby.

As we have seen, Abingdon Abbey was probably responsible for bringing the navigation on its present course through the town. The Abbey was founded in the seventh century; there is a story in the Abbey Chronicle telling of an early dispute between the Abingdon monks and the inhabitants of Oxford, when both parties laid claim to a meadow which was bounded by two streams of the Thames. The monks adopted a strange method of settling the question: taking a round shield, they placed upon it a sheaf of corn, in which was fixed a lighted taper; and having launched the shield and its burden on the river, they permitted it to drift away with the current. Soon it reached the point where the waters divided, and floated off down one of the two channels, indicating to the satisfaction of both parties which channel was henceforth to be regarded as the principal and therefore the boundary stream. (In fact the monks won their claim.) The shield and sheaf were, incidentally, symbols originally used by the pre-Christian Saxons to commemorate the legendary King Sheaf, father of Scyld, who had appeared in an oarless ship with a sheaf of corn for a pillow.

Culham Lock and lock cut by-pass the old course of the river, which falls by way of several weirs into Sutton Pool. A mill spanned the stream near the Fish Inn at Sutton Courtenay, and a pound lock was built there during the early seventeenth century, probably by the miller. The lock was unusual in that it was partly beneath the ground floor of the mill, and could only be used at the expense of water from the milling business. Consequently a heavy toll was always levied by the miller, the heaviest single toll on the Thames: thirty shillings per sixty tons in 1774. This lock was superseded when the new lock and cut were opened in 1809, and the mill has vanished. Today the United Kingdom Atomic Energy Authority have an outfall here, to return water to the Thames which they have used at their nearby Harwell premises. Similarly Didcot Power Station, a short distance further down the river, uses Thames water.

Clifton Hampden Bridge was built in 1865. The Barley Mow Inn is adjacent; Jerome K. Jerome stayed here while he was writing *Three Men In A*

The Barley Mow Inn, Clifton Hampden circa 1877 (*Henry Taunt*).

*Boat* (published in 1889). In the book he pays the inn this tribute: 'It is, without exception, I should say, the quaintest, most old-world inn up the river . . . Its low-pitched gables and thatched roof and latticed windows give it quite a story-book appearance, while inside it is still more once-upon-a-timeyfied.' The inn was subsequently enlarged but was badly damaged by fire in 1975. The author of *Three Men In A Boat* is buried in Ewelme churchyard, not far away.

Shortly beyond Clifton comes Burcot, the hamlet once made famous by the Commission. The Riverside Hotel affords the only landing place here. Two miles below is Day's Lock, which acquired that name only in the 1820s; before that it was known as Dorchester or Little Wittenham Lock. Mr Day's identity does not seem to have been discovered, even by the tireless Thacker. If you have time to leave the river here, walk the few hundred yards across the fields to the earthworks on the north bank, known as the Dyke Hills, that are the site of an Iron Age settlement. The River Thame flows into the Thames just below Day's Lock. It is not navigable by motor cruisers, but canoes and similar craft can travel up it for some distance. The confluence was supposed to be the place where the names Thames and Isis combined to form *Tamesis*.

Shillingford Bridge, a mile below, was built about 1830, but there may have been a bridge here as long ago as Roman times. After Shillingford the river soon reaches Benson Lock, where the towpath once again changes sides and obliges the walker to make a detour. Soon the openwork spire of St Peter's Church indicates the nearness of Wallingford.

A Salter's steamer at Shillingford Bridge, circa 1948 (*Thomas Photos*).

Leland called Wallingford Bridge 'a large Thing of Stone over the *Tamise*', and so it is, boasting numerous arches of mediæval construction (the actual date when it was built is obscure). In 1809 it was widened by about four feet on the upstream side, with the result that one face has rounded arches with keystones and bosses, and the other still has the original pointed arches.

A short way below Wallingford Bridge stood Chalmore Hole Lock, which was built in 1838, but was found to be unnecessary (the fall was only eighteen inches) and was removed in 1883. In *Three Men In A Boat* Jerome tells the story of rowing down this reach one evening without realising that the lock had been removed, and constantly expecting to arrive at it: 'I recollected the lock myself. I had been through it twice. Where were we? What had happened to us? I began to think it must all be a dream . . .'

If you are on foot, on the way out of Wallingford you may confront somebody mowing his lawn or weeding his flower-bed, for the towpath leads you quite officially through a number of private gardens. This is an easy reach for the boater (there are six and a half clear miles between Benson and Cleeve Locks), but for the walker there are unusual exertions. The towpath crosses again by Fair Mile Hospital, but with patience and a stout stick it is possible to fight your way through the undergrowth to Moulsford Railway Bridge, where a track leads up to the Waterloo Inn and Moulsford village. This bridge is very different from the iron structures carrying the railway at Nuneham and Appleford, for it is handsomely built of brick and was designed

A side-arch of Wallingford Bridge, showing the original mediaeval ribs and the nineteenth century widening.

by Brunel, architect of the Great Western Railway. In Moulsford itself stands Hobbs's boathouse (not directly connected with the Henley firm of the same name) housing some handsome Thames skiffs still in fine order.

If you want dinner or a bed for the night, the Beetle and Wedge Hotel in Moulsford can provide both; or you can go on to the Olde Leatherne Bottel (as it is spelt by the proprietor) on the opposite bank at South Stoke. There is a wider choice of hotels and pubs in Goring, now only a short way off. If you are walking, take care that you do not miss your way just before you get into the town; the towpath turns away from the river, and in the dark it is easy to get lost here. In front of you now is Goring Gap, where the Thames burrows its way between the chalk hills of the Chilterns on one side and the Berkshire Downs on the other, to reach the easier going of the London clay below.

The Thames below Goring.

Goring Lock has for many years been provided with three pairs of gates (as have Cookham, Boulter's and Chertsey). The extra pair are positioned about one third of the way down the chamber, and can be used to make a smaller lock and so save water; they are, however, scarcely ever used.

Goring Gap and the hills on either side recede as you continue your journey down the river. If you are on foot, cross the bridge and take the main road from Streatley towards Pangbourne, to avoid another ferry-less crossing (and to get a good view of the Gap just as you are leaving Streatley). You can rejoin the river by Basildon Church. The Childe-Beale Trust has its premises here; it is chiefly concerned with giving a home to various species of birds, but it also houses an incongruous collection of statuary (gathered by Gilbert Beale) which stands in peculiar isolation by the river, far from habitation.

The outskirts of Pangbourne suggest a seaside resort rather than a Thames town, with rows of Victorian villas showing the influence of the Brighton Pavilion, and little lawns and steps ornamented with geraniums leading down to the river and the residents' launches. The River Pang flows into the Thames almost unnoticed just below the weir. Whitchurch Toll Bridge (built in the 1880s) leads to Whitchurch village, quieter than Pangbourne but even more exclusive.

By the Church of St James the Less in Pangbourne stands Church Cottage. Here lived and died the creator of the Water Rat, the Mole and Mr Toad: Kenneth Grahame, author of *The Wind in the Willows*, one of the best known of all river books.

Kenneth Grahame was born in Scotland, the son of a lawyer, in 1859, but after his mother's death five years later he and his brothers and sister were brought up by the Thames at Cookham Dean, near Marlow. His maternal grandmother looked after them, and her house bounded the river. When Kenneth was nine he was sent to St Edward's School in Oxford, where he did well at academic work and sport, and learnt to canoe on the Upper River.

He left school in 1876 and wanted to go to Oxford, but instead his family arranged a clerkship for him in the Bank of England. While living in London he met Frederick James Furnivall, an energetic radical and scholar who was also a passionate enthusiast for sculling. Furnivall ran a highly successful working men's rowing club on the Thames, and conducted a ferocious campaign against the Amateur Rowing Association for excluding artisans from its competitions. Someone wrote of him: 'Dr Furnivall will ask you if you can scull. If you say "No" he will take you up the river to teach you. If you say "Yes" he will take you up the river to keep you in practice. He will take you anyhow.' He took Kenneth Grahame.

Meanwhile Grahame (thanks to Furnivall's encouragement) was writing

Kenneth Grahame, by J. S. Sargent, 1912
(*Bodleian Library*).

and getting published. Two collections of childhood sketches, *The Golden Age* and *Dream Days*, were commissioned from him by W. E. Henley, the editor whose brilliant circle of writers was dubbed by Max Beerbohm 'Henley's Regatta'. Grahame was also doing well in his profession, and by 1898 had risen to be Secretary to the Bank of England. The following year he married Elspeth Thomson, stepdaughter of a Liberal M.P., a dominant woman who bore him a son, Alastair, in 1900.

From babyhood Alastair Grahame was nicknamed 'Mouse'. He was blind in his right eye and squinted with his left, and was awkward and painfully shy. But Elspeth was convinced that her son was brilliant, and his nursery became the focus of their life. In 1906 they left London and moved back to Grahame's childhood landscape by the Thames, taking 'Mayfield', a house at Cookham Dean.

By this date Kenneth Grahame had already begun to tell his son bedtime stories. They apparently began on the boy's fourth birthday in 1904, a day when there was a flood of tears so great that only the promise of a story about anything he liked could quell them. Alastair chose a mole, a giraffe, and a rat, and the story began—and went on night after night, until the giraffe had been replaced by a Toad, and *The Wind in the Willows* was born.

Three years later Grahame was persuaded to make the tale into a book.

Reluctantly he began. The Thames was not far from the house where he worked, and in any case he knew it intimately, particularly the reaches between Cookham and Pangbourne, with the great mansions of Mapledurham and Harleyford standing near the water to suggest Toad Hall, and perhaps the sinister gloom of Quarry Wood at Cookham Dean to give birth to the Wild Wood. And, of course, there was Grahame's own love of sculling: 'Believe me, my young friend, there is *nothing*—absolutely nothing—half so much worth doing as simply messing about in boats.'

*The Wind in the Willows* was published (after some difficulty) in 1908. At first the critical reception was mixed: the *Times* wrote 'As a contribution to natural history, the work is negligible'. But it sold well and was reprinted three times in the following year. Meanwhile the Grahames' lease had run out at Cookham, and they moved to Blewbury on the Berkshire Downs. Alastair was sent first to Rugby and then to Eton, but he was desperately unhappy and had to be taken away from both schools. He went up to Christ Church, Oxford, in 1918, but once again seemed miserable. Two years later he was found dead on the railway line near Port Meadow after being struck by a train. The verdict was accidental death, but many people suspected suicide.

Strangely his parents' reaction was almost one of relief; he had been the focus of their hopes, but it had become painfully obvious that he would never fulfil them. Elspeth shocked the neighbourhood by selling her son's clothes at a jumble sale, then she and Kenneth took a Mediterranean cruise and returned to live at Church Cottage, Pangbourne, in 1924.

It is a modest but handsome house, with the old village lock-up for a tool shed. Grahame was respected in the neighbourhood but took little part in local affairs; Elspeth attracted more notice, and is still remembered as an eccentric. The Grahames were not lavish with their money; they had no telephone or servants, and could sometimes be seen on the front porch eating lunch out of a paper bag; but they drank a lot of champagne and port.

By 1932 Grahame was in his seventy-third year and was suffering from high blood-pressure. On the fifth of July he walked by his beloved Thames, mixed the salad at dinner as he always did, and died at six o'clock the following morning. The funeral was in the church next to his house, but he is buried in Oxford, in St Cross churchyard, a few yards from the river Cherwell.

HARDWICK AND MAPLEDURHAM

Downstream of Pangbourne, river and railway (which have run together for many miles) part company, and there is relief from the feeling that both are making with indecent haste for London. The towpath skirts flat open fields

Hardwick House.

on the south bank, but across the river on the Oxfordshire side rises a wooded slope, and through the trees may be glimpsed first one, and then (a short way along) another Elizabethan mansion, each as fine an embodiment of Toad Hall as one could wish for.

The first is Hardwick House, late Tudor in general style, but altered at various times since Elizabeth I slept in the medallioned bedroom that bears her name. The manor remained in the hands of the Lybbe family, whose guest the Queen had been, until the late nineteenth century when Hardwick was sold to Sir Charles Day Rose, M.P. Sir Charles built at Hardwick an enclosed court for the playing of that rare game of 'Royal Tennis', and his emblem, the rose, can be seen decorating the walls and iron gates of the house and estate.

Behind Hardwick House a road leads through an avenue of sycamores to the eastern edge of the estate. There it becomes a chalky track, still high above the level of the river, and eventually this reaches the second of these two riverside manors, Mapledurham House, with the church of St Margaret and the tiny village beside it.

The Manor of Mapledurham has seemed to many visitors to be a strangely well-preserved relic of feudalism. The main road by-passes the village, and no bridge connects it with the twentieth century community on the opposite bank. The house remains in the hands of a member of the family that built it in 1588, the Blounts. The half-timbered outhouses beside the mansion are the remnants of its mediæval predecessor. The weatherboarded mill is one of

Mapledurham House.

the oldest on the river; when it ceased to grind corn earlier in this century, it was adapted for a time to pump water for the estate reservoirs and drive the dynamo that provided the Manor's electricity.

To judge by its appearance the whole village might have stood still since the time of its most famous vicar, the Reverend Lord Augustus Fitz-Clarence, who was one of William IV's ten children by his mistress Mrs Jordan, a celebrated Irish comic actress. For some reason the parish of Mapledurham was the one on which Lord Augustus, or his father, had set his heart; but the incumbent was reluctant to leave, and was only eventually prised out in 1829 by the offer of a bishopric. The King gave his natural son's parish church a clock which bears his initials, and a barrel-organ that could play twelve tunes. William was not the first monarch to notice Mapledurham. The patron of the living is Eton College, to which it was granted by Henry VI. Many of the Vicars have therefore been Etonians, among them John Burton, the eighteenth century author of a tract on the navigation of the Thames.

Mapledurham House is principally known for its history as a Catholic haven. The Blounts were Catholic and have remained so, and the house has many relics of persecution: a priest-hole, a trap-door, remains of secret passages. The church has a curious 'closed aisle' used by the Catholic Blounts

93

as their own private chapel and family vault, and partitioned from the Anglican remainder of the church.

One of the English Catholics to whom Mapledurham gave hospitality was the poet Alexander Pope, whose friendship with the Blount family is well documented. He first met the sisters Martha and Teresa Blount in Reading when he was nineteen, they seventeen and nineteen respectively. A firm friendship and a ream of letters followed, and Pope became a frequent visitor to the house until, perhaps because he declared himself to be in love with the younger sister and so offended the elder, the friendship was soured. But before that rift he wrote these lines for Teresa, on the occasion of her returning home to Mapledurham after a stay in London for the coronation of King George I:

> She went to plain work, and to purling brooks,
> Old fashioned halls, dull aunts and croaking rooks.
> She went from opera, park, assembly, play,
> To morning walks, and prayers three hours a day.

John Galsworthy too wrote, though less succinctly, about Mapledurham. In the *Forsyte Saga*, Soames Forsyte has a mansion called 'The Shelter' at Mapledurham, and the closing pages of *Swan Song* depict his burial under a crab-apple tree in the graveyard there, within hearing of the river that is, to Galsworthy, the emblem of essential change.

There are of course no actual mortal remains of Soames in Mapledurham churchyard, but its memorials are none the less interesting. On the north wall of the church near the choir stalls a tablet commemorates a rector of Purley, the parish on the other side of the river: 'He lost his life crossing the Thames after doing an act of kindness in taking the evening service at Mapledurham, December 20th 1914.' And the Rose family of Hardwick House are buried here: there is a memorial in the churchyard to Sir Charles Rose, Bart., M.P., who 'died April 20th 1913 from the effects of an aeroplane flight'.

It is not possible to cross the river at Mapledurham Lock. The village can only be reached from Hardwick and from the Whitchurch to Caversham road; the towpath remains on the other side, leads to Purley, and then stops, obstructed in turn by the Purley caravan club, the Purley cruiser club, and a railway embankment that rises sheer from the water. The walker who decides not to face the peril of crossing these has to extricate himself from Purley and find the road to Tilehurst.

Purley is a community chiefly made up of wooden dwellings that have somewhat outlasted their allotted life-span; they have undergone a profusion of improvements and have acquired permanent status. The bungalows are dwarfed and are sometimes completely obscured by the cars and cruisers parked outside the front doors, while the roads are an untarred maze.

After Tilehurst (where a convenient footbridge over the railway leads back

Mapledurham Mill.

to the towpath) the threat of the impeding town recedes for a few fields' length, until Reading's Thames-side Promenade begins. Then the path broadens into a strip of well-organised parkland, the villas of Caversham appear on the north bank, and the startling white double span of Caversham Bridge comes into sight. You have reached Reading.

# VI

# Commissioners and Conservators

Just above Reading Bridge is Nugent House, the modern office block which since 1973 has been the headquarters of the Thames Conservancy, now the Thames Conservancy Division of the Thames Water Authority. The Chief Engineer's department has been here for much longer, in a neighbouring building, and here also is the workshop for the navigation district between Wallingford and Marlow. So this seems to be a good place to pause from our journey down the river, and consider the history of the various authorities which at different times have had charge of the Thames.

After the Oxford-Burcot Commission of the early seventeenth century had done its work, the river languished for over a century. Even these early Commissioners had only 'improved' fourteen miles of the Thames; elsewhere the old weirs stood, or crumbled, or were set up afresh. There was no one to build any more pound locks, or to take any other form of action to improve matters.

Some slight provision for control of the Thames was made in 1695 by an Act establishing the Justices of the Peace in the riverside counties as authorities for regulating the navigation and fixing tolls, but this did not have much effect. A more important step was taken in 1751 when Parliament set up the first permanent general authority to control the navigation above Staines. This authority was made up of local landowners and other influential persons, but had no mandate to do anything much more than fix the rates of tolls. Then in 1770 another Act strengthened these feeble powers, and brought into being the body that came to be known as the Thames Commissioners.

### THE THAMES COMMISSIONERS OF 1770

Under the 1770 Act there were to be well over 600 Commissioners, with authority over the river from Cricklade to London Bridge. The following people were qualified to be Commissioners: anyone with an estate, the annual value of which exceeded £100, anywhere in the seven riverside counties

James Lowe, lock-keeper at Day's Lock, 1904 (*Henry Taunt*).

above Staines; representatives of Oxford University; Mayors and Recorders of the principal riverside towns; Members of Parliament representing constituencies in the riverside counties, and Members who merely lived there; the Corporation of the City of London; clergy from riparian parishes (and from Westminster, St Paul's Cathedral and Eton); the commissioners and proprietors of the River Wey navigation; and various other persons. But a quorum for meetings was only eleven people.

The unwieldy membership was made up for by the considerable powers granted to the new authority, which could make and acquire towpaths compulsorily, purchase the old flash weirs, and (very important) 'erect and maintain pounds or turnpikes where (flash) locks or weirs are now made use of'. And with very little delay major improvements were begun. Two regular 'flashes' were to be let through the weirs each week, on Tuesday and Friday, and the Commissioners fixed the exact hour at which the weirkeepers and millers were to open the sluices, a great improvement on the old uncertainty when barges would be kept waiting at the miller's whim. And most important of all, the Commissioners began to build a series of pound locks, the first to be constructed on the Thames for 140 years.

The first eight new locks were built during 1772-3 between Maidenhead

97

Shiplake Lock, built 1772-3, with wooden fencing.

and Reading: they were Boulter's, Marlow, Temple, Hurley, Hambleden, Marsh, Shiplake and Sonning. These were not the sturdy stone chambers of Iffley, Sandford and the Swift Ditch, for money was short and stone expensive. So timber was used, and the locks were fenced with an open frame of wood which proved poor at withstanding the buffeting of the barges. Ten years later all eight locks were in a parlous state, and most of them had to be rebuilt. Meanwhile the flash weirs adjoining the locks were fastened up, though by a provision of the 1770 Act their owners had to be compensated heavily by the Commissioners.

Below Boulter's Lock at Maidenhead nothing was done, and for a long time nothing could be done, for conflict had arisen between the Commissioners and the City of London, which had for many centuries claimed some kind of jurisdiction over the whole Thames, and certainly reckoned to be the navigation authority below Staines. In 1771 an agreement between the City and the Commissioners prevented either party from erecting any new locks or weirs below Maidenhead. In 1774 another Act partly resolved the deadlock by restoring to the City the jurisdiction over the river from Staines to London Bridge, although the City did very little to improve this district until it built Teddington Lock in 1811. Meanwhile Maidenhead to Staines remained a no-man's land.

During the 1780s the Commissioners acquired the services of Robert Mylne, who became their principal surveyor. Mylne was the son of a Scottish architect and was well known himself both as architect and engineer. His

98

work for the Commissioners was untiring and covered many years. Late in the 1780s he surveyed the Thames and reported that much of it was almost unnavigable. He was particularly concerned that the old weirs should not continue in private ownership, and wrote: 'The Working of the Weirs ought to go hand in hand with the Pounding of the Water by the New Locks.' He attacked the ancient practice of employing the neighbouring miller or his servant as lock keeper, under which system the miller's interests invariably took first place. He also recommended that the fishing rights at the weirs and locks should be purchased by the Commissioners, so that the lock keepers should not let the interests of the fishery owners come before the navigation. The Commissioners took his advice and purchased the rights, and fishing at locks and weirs still belongs to the Thames Conservancy.

The opening of the Thames & Severn Canal in 1789 made the improvement of the river navigation a matter of urgency, as the Upper Thames now had a new importance as a through route to the West and the Midlands. Six pound locks were built above Oxford, the first in that district. St John's and Rushey Locks were opened in 1790, built of stone under the charge of a contractor named Nock, who also constructed Pinkhill Lock in the following year. Meanwhile Osney and Godstow Locks were being built by Daniel Harris the Oxford Gaoler, who was a carpenter by profession. The Commissioners were ridiculed for employing him, but he seems to have done his work well enough, using gangs of felons from the prison to help him; one is reminded of occasions today when prisoners and Borstal boys help with waterway restoration projects.

More locks were built by the Commissioners below Oxford: Mapledurham in 1777, Caversham in 1778, Cleeve, Goring and Whitchurch in 1788. (Culham Lock and cut were not built until 1809). These locks were generally of timber with open sides, and cost a little over £1,000 each. Benson Lock was built with the help of 'Low Country men', presumably Dutchmen skilled in the construction of pound locks. The labourers worked long hours for low wages, 5 am to 7 pm for less than 1½d per hour. But they were not kept short of refreshment, for an item in the accounts for the building of Cleeve Lock records 'Beere & Gin gave the men working in the water and Pumping a Nights'.

Other improvements were needed besides the erection of pound locks. An Act of 1795 gave the Commissioners compulsory purchase powers by which they might achieve a 'free and continuous' towing path, though they were not permitted to take land where a house, garden or orchard already occupied it. Perhaps chiefly because of this restriction, a continuous path was not achieved and never has been. In 1796 the Commissioners, following Mylne's advice, decided to build houses at all the locks and compel the keepers to live in them.

Opening the sluices at Shifford Lock. All Thames locks above Godstow are operated manually.

## CANAL MANIA

The 1795 Act gave the Commissioners power to build more locks, but still not below Maidenhead without notice to the Corporation of London. Romney Lock at Windsor was the first to be built in this district, in 1797, and there were plans to build others. But these were vigorously opposed by riparian landowners who feared that the new locks and weirs would cause floods, and by those parties who championed the ever growing cause of the canals.

The canal age was well under way, and as the nineteenth century dawned the Oxford, Thames & Severn, and Grand Junction Canals had been opened (the latter connecting the Midlands to London by a direct route independent of the Thames). Navigation on them was a less troublesome business than on the river, for they had no tiresome flash weirs and their tolls were less exorbitant (and did not have to be paid lock by lock). Why then, argued the canal propagandists, should not the Thames itself be by-passed and canals dug to take its traffic, or at least to cut off some of its longer meanders? Many such by-pass canals were suggested, among them waterways from Lechlade to Abingdon, from Reading to Monkey Island, and from Boulter's Lock to Isleworth. The Commissioners became anxious, and by 1810 they had borrowed £66,800 to help build more locks and make other improvements, for it was imperative that traffic and revenue should not be diverted from the river. A particular threat came from a proposed canal between Abingdon and Marsworth (on the Grand Junction near Tring), for together with the North Wilts and the Wilts & Berks Canal this would have provided a route from the Thames & Severn Canal to London without using a yard of Thames water. It was vital, as one Commissioner wrote, that all interested parties should 'unite in resisting the confederacy and conspiracy against old Father Thames, and saving that royal river from its meditated destruction'.

At last the City of London began to do something constructive in the part of the Thames that was under its control. In 1811 it built Teddington Lock, and this was followed in the next four years by locks at Sunbury, Chertsey, Shepperton, Penton Hook and Molesey. The Commissioners, too, were active, and during the succeeding years they built all the remaining locks now to be found between Oxford and Staines. In 1817 Bell Weir Lock was opened, Clifton and Old Windsor followed in 1822, and then came Cookham (1830), Boveney (1838) and Bray (1845), the latter at a cost of £2,887. Little by little the canal threat receded and eventually vanished; and indeed the canals themselves were soon hard pressed, like the Thames, by a new adversary.

'THAT MOST USELESS AND MISCHIEVOUS PROJECT'

In 1834 a Bill to establish the Great Western Railway came before Parliament. The new invention was clearly going to be a menace to the river, for if a railway line were opened along the Thames Valley and thence to Bristol, the waterborne commercial traffic would be seriously threatened by a swifter and probably cheaper form of transport. The Commissioners accordingly spent £1,500 in organising opposition to the Bill, and it was thrown out by a large majority. But it came before Parliament again, and in 1841 'that most useless and mischievous project', as the commissioners had dubbed the Great Western Railway, became a reality.

Soon the Commissioners were taking desperate steps to make river transport competitive with the new railway; in 1844 they reduced all tolls by twenty per cent, and in 1850 tolls were abandoned completely at Abingdon and Old Windsor locks. But the inevitable had happened: the railway had soon taken much of the river traffic, and the main line to Bristol was already being augmented by branches to many of the riverside towns. In 1853 the Commissioners took the drastic measure of reducing lock keepers' wages by up to one half, although the keepers were allowed to compensate themselves by retaining the tolls from the increasing pleasure traffic. In 1854 the Commissioners could only pay two per cent interest on their bonds, in 1857 one per cent. The barge traffic continued to decline, and in the first five months of 1862 only nine vessels passed from the Thames & Severn Canal into the Thames at Inglesham. In 1863 half a per cent interest was paid. In 1864 all new works were abandoned unless funds were in hand to meet them, and the river was virtually left to rot. In 1865 it was reported that 'the gates (of the locks) and weirs are all so leaky that they do not sufficiently store the water, and the gates of many of them are in such a bad condition that they can hardly be opened.' Barge owners often had 'to precede their boats twenty miles and to return the same distance, to solicit and pay dear for water to bring them over the shoals and bars'. The river once again came under the sway of the old adversaries of navigation: a contemporary barge-master reported that 'the millers stand and laugh at our men when they cannot go on, after they have paid for getting the water ... At Sandford Lock the miller's man stood and laughed at our man and said: "Thank you for bringing the water," and we had to lie there till the next flash.'

Other navigations besides the Thames were in sore straits from railway competition, often with disastrous results, for during the latter half of the nineteenth century many waterways became totally derelict and unnavigable. Some are still in that state, and others are only being reopened today thanks to the work of voluntary societies. The Thames navigation had an exceedingly narrow escape from the same fate; that it did survive was due to a combination of circumstances.

The City of London urgently needed £30,000 for repairs on its section of the river, but could not raise the money, and so in 1856 resigned its claim to jurisdiction over the Thames. The next year the Crown granted control of the lower Thames to a new authority, a Board of Conservancy, which came into being on 1 March 1857, and lived until 31 March 1974.

THE FIRST CONSERVATORS

The new Thames Conservancy was responsible for the river from Staines down to Yantlet Creek just above the mouth of the Medway. Although the City of London had relinquished its control, it was well represented on the new Board, which was made up of the Lord Mayor of London and two Aldermen from the City, four members of the City's Common Council, the Deputy Master of Trinity House (the pilotage and lighthouse authority), two nominees of the Admiralty, one nominee of the Government's Trade and Foreign Plantations Committee, and one nominee of Trinity House. Over the years the number of Conservators was increased as other interests needed to be represented on the Board.

Meanwhile the Thames Commissioners continued to be responsible for the river above Staines, and they were (as we have seen) operating under extreme difficulties. In any case they were ill equipped to deal with the crisis, with the unwieldy nature of their membership and their inadequate statutory powers, so in 1866 they were disbanded, and their powers were transferred to the Thames Conservators, to whose number five more were added. So in 1866 the Conservancy found itself in charge of the whole river from Cricklade to Yantlet Creek.

There was an appalling shortage of funds, but by 1880 almost all the locks and weirs above Staines had been reconstructed or adequately repaired. Meanwhile the Conservators were fighting a battle against pollution, with some success, for by 1874 the only towns which continued to discharge sewage into the river above the Metropolitan Water Companies' intakes were Oxford, Abingdon, Reading and Windsor, and by 1880 even these places had built proper sewage works. Below the intakes, however, Kingston, Richmond and the Metropolitan Board of Works still poured untreated sewage into the Thames.

The Thames Act of 1883 marked a step of a different kind, for it provided for the registration of steam launches navigating the river above Kew Bridge. In 1885 registration was made compulsory for all pleasure boats. In 1889 twelve thousand craft (including houseboats) were registered.

During the 1890s the Conservators were turning their attention to improvements above Oxford, where flash weirs were still more plentiful than pound locks. New locks were built between 1890 and 1898 at Northmoor, Radcot, Grafton and Shifford.

In 1900 a Royal Commission was instituted to consider the best means of developing the Port of London. In 1902 it recommended that the control of the tidal river (below Teddington) should be taken from the Conservancy and vested in a new authority specially created to manage the affairs of shipping and the docks. The Conservators raised strong objections, and even tried to increase their powers, but the Board of Trade was adamant, and although the fight was protracted until 1908, in that year the Port of London Act was passed. This provided for the creation of the Port of London Authority, to which were transferred (as from 31 March 1909) the rights, powers and duties of the Thames Conservators in respect of the Thames

The Conservators of the River Thames on their annual inspection, pre-1914. Lord Desborough stands, sixth from the left, with one hand in a pocket (*R. R. Bolland collection*).

below a point about 265 yards downstream of the gates of Teddington New Lock.

THE DESBOROUGH YEARS

The creation of the Port of London Authority was a serious blow to the Conservators, who had lost the prestige of being the sole body responsible for the Thames. They had also lost their London office premises, for the new P. L. A. took over the Conservancy's Victoria Embankment building. Homeless, the Conservators debated whether they should move their headquarters to Reading or remain in London. By a large majority they decided on London. The Chairman, Lord Desborough, regretted this decision so much that he offered his resignation, but his fellow board members persuaded him to remain in office. (The Conservancy eventually moved to Reading in 1973.)

Lord Desborough was the longest-serving Conservancy Chairman, holding office from 1904 to 1937, and was himself no mean river athlete. While an undergraduate at Balliol he rowed in two Boat Races, and was later the only man to compete for the Grand Challenge Cup at Henley while a Member of Parliament. He also rowed stroke in an eight which crossed the English

Channel, and sculled in a crew of three from Oxford to London in twenty-two consecutive hours, including the time taken at locks. He won the Amateur Punting Championship for three years in succession, remaining unbeaten, and twice swam the pool below Niagara Falls. He was involved with a multitude of causes, and at one time was serving on no less than 115 committees, but the Thames was always a principle concern to him.

In the early days of Lord Desborough's chairmanship of the Conservancy, money was extremely short. Nevertheless by 1927 the Thames above Oxford had been almost totally modernized. Among other improvements, pound locks were built to replace flash weirs at Eynsham and King's; Medley Weir survived some four years more. Lord Desborough retired from the Chairmanship in 1937, and in the same year Eaton Hastings Weir, the last of the flash weirs, was removed.

When a new channel was dug at Weybridge in the early 1930s it was named the Desborough Cut. Lord Desborough died in 1945 at the age of 89.

THE MECHANISATION OF LOCKS

One of the biggest projects undertaken by the Thames Conservancy in the years after the 1939–45 war was the mechanization of all the locks from Teddington to Godstow. In 1956 an experimental electrical-mechanical system was installed at Mapledurham Lock, and a similar system was put in soon afterwards at Cookham. In 1961 the first hydraulic lock gate mechanism was installed at Shiplake, and this was the system that came to be adopted at all the remaining locks.

The hydraulic equipment was built by the appropriately named Lockheed company, and operates at a pressure of about 750 lb per square inch, the pressure being generated by a small rotary pump driven by a 2 h.p. 3-phase motor controlled from the pedestals at either end of the lock. This equipment opens and shuts the lock gates at the touch of a lever, and also operates the sluices which raise and lower the water in the lock.

Eventually all the remaining locks from Teddington to Godstow were mechanized, the work being done at eight locks each winter during the 1960s. Motors up to 4 hp and pressures up to 1,000 lb per square inch are in use where there are bigger gates and heavier sluices. If the electric power fails (or if a crew need to work the lock when the keeper is off duty) the hand wheel on each pedestal can be used to drive the hydraulic pump.

For the time being no automatic locks are to be installed above Godstow, and at the remaining locks the keeper turns wheels on the gates to operate the sluices, and the gates themselves are moved by stout wooden balance beams.

In its latter days the Thames Conservancy changed the system of collecting

The automated gates at Benson Lock.

revenue. Until 1967, besides the registration fee for each boat, a small toll had to be paid at every lock passed. In that year an all-in fee was adopted, and it has risen sharply ever since. Licences have to be obtained for the time being from the Conservancy's Reading headquarters.

Despite mechanization, a resident keeper is still needed for each of the forty-four locks above Teddington, and there are also thirty relief keepers who do duty during the resident keeper's days off or illness. 'Summer assistants' are recruited to help when traffic is at its heaviest, and many of these are female, though women are not yet employed as full-time lock keepers on the grounds that the duties are too heavy, especially at the old rymer and paddle weirs.

The weir is still the centre of the lock keeper's working life, and he is first and foremost a weir keeper with a duty to keep the water level as near as possible to the correct 'head water' mark for the lock. Though it is the responsibility of all lock keepers to watch the water levels, there are also special automatic gauging stations at Cricklade, Eynsham, Day's, Bray and Teddington, and an experimental 'flow' gauging station on the Clifton reach measures the speed of the current. There are also thirty-eight gauging stations on the tributaries.

Thames Conservancy steam launch *Donola* at Reading Bridge (*R. R. Bolland*).

In the winter there is often too much water in the river, particularly now that agricultural land is being drained more effectively, so that rainwater which used to seep slowly into the Thames now rushes in through culverts. Conversely there is increasing concern at the lack of water in the river during the summer, since two thirds of London's water supply comes from the Thames, and at present a scheme is being developed to pump water into the river in dry seasons from boreholes in the chalk and limestone of the Thames catchment area. Pilot bores for the scheme were made in the Lambourn Valley during the 1960s.

Besides being an expert on controlling the water level, the lock keeper must be a good gardener, for a high standard of lock gardens is expected by the Conservancy. The annual lock gardens competition was instituted in 1898, and for many years until 1968 the party of Conservators doing the judging used to travel in the elegant steam launch *Donola*, which is now in the National Maritime Museum at Greenwich. A more frequent visitor to each lock was, and is, the patrol launch of the navigation district carrying the navigation officers, who keep a wary eye on boats and crews and also act as supervisors to the lock keepers.

The keeper's job involves dealing with boaters and other river users, but for much of the year he is in isolation. Few of the lock houses are close to villages or towns, and in times of flood the shopping may have to be done by

Repairing the lock gates at Bray.

boat. There may also be severe frosts or floods to contend with. But large numbers of people still apply to be keepers, and there is no difficulty in filling the available jobs.

Nowadays a keeper deals almost exclusively with pleasure boats, for the years since the 1939–45 war have seen the almost total disappearance of commercial traffic on the Thames above Teddington. In 1945, 248,500 tons were carried by barge on the non-tidal river, but by 1971 this had dropped to a mere 17,300 tons. The decline continued as grain and timber carrying around the Weybridge, Walton and Kingston districts ceased and traders went out of business, and the coal traffic to Surbiton and Hampton was transferred to the roads. In 1974 a mere 1,644 tons were carried, mainly dredgings from the Metropolitan Water Board's filter beds and a small quantity of building materials carried from Hampton Wick to Eel Pie Island. There is a growing movement in Britain to revive water cargo carrying, but it has yet to have an effect on the non-tidal Thames.

THE THAMES WATER AUTHORITY

In 1973 the Government decided to form Water Authorities which would control rivers, water supplies from source to tap, sewage, and (where applicable) navigation; they were to replace virtually all existing water, sewage and navigation authorities in Britain. A powerful lobby eventually saved the country's canals from this fate, and the British Waterways Board has continued to control them, but the Thames Conservancy, together with other river boards, fell victim to the axe of reorganisation.

The Conservators fought hard to retain their control over the Thames. When the reorganisation proposals were first put forward in 1971 they declared 'The Thames Conservancy has been in existence for 114 years and it is generally acknowledged nationally and internationally that the River Thames is one of the best managed rivers in the world . . . The Conservators are conscious of their great responsibility to the River Thames and believe that their standard of management has measured up to the importance of their task today and tomorrow.' But it was to no avail, and on 1 April 1974 (the significance of the date did not escape comment) the Conservators laid down their jurisdiction and were disbanded. Their powers were vested in the Thames Water Authority, a vast organisation controlled from London and including the old Metropolitan Water Board and all the other water boards in the Thames and Lea catchment areas.

The Thames Conservancy Division of the Authority (as it is now called) is still housed at Reading, and outwardly the river shows little sign of a change in management. But there is concern about the future of the Thames; for navigation, always a principal concern of the Conservators is 'only a sideline' of the new Authority, as one observer wryly put it. Whether the Thames Water Authority will equal the achievements of its predecessors remains to be seen.

# VII

# Gin on the River: Reading to Teddington

If you want to see one of the best parts of Reading, turn off the Thames and go under the bridge by the gasworks, along the lowest reach of the River Kennet, which in turn leads to the Kennet & Avon Canal. Along here by the hissing gas-pipes are three waterside pubs, the Jolly Anglers, the Thames Tavern and the Fisherman's Cottage, all linked by a row of attractive though now rather dilapidated terraced houses. Here also is Blake's Lock, which is controlled by the Thames Conservancy and has a resident lock keeper. The Thames Commissioners looked after it before the Conservancy, presumably because it led to busy wharves served by Thames barges.

For many centuries Reading was an important centre of distribution for the neighbourhood, and when an Act of 1715 permitted navigation from that town up the Kennet to Newbury, the Reading bargemen believed their livelihood to be threatened, as Newbury would be able to receive goods at its own wharves. During the next ten years the Kennet was made navigable by pound locks and cuts, but mobs of Reading men attacked the works and threw stones at barges, and in July 1725 a Maidenhead bargemaster, Peter Darvall, received this letter:

> Mr Darvell wee Bargemen of Redding thought to Aquaint you before 'tis too Late Dam you if you work a bote any more to Newbury wee will kill you if ever you come any more this way wee was very near shooting you last time wee went with to pistolls and was not too Minnets too Late, the first time Your Boat Lays at Redding Loaded Dam you wee will bore hols in her and sink her so Dont come to starve our Fammeleys and our Masters for Dam You if You do we will send you short home for you have no aceation to come to teak the bred out of Oure Childrens Mouths wee made an atempt wen Your boat Lay at bleaks bridg only Your men must beene all drownd so teake Worning before 'tis too late, for Dam You if ever you come we will doo it from Wee Bargemen.

Blake's Lock, on the Kennet at Reading.

Despite such bloodthirstiness, navigation up the Kennet to Newbury became well established, and when in 1810 the Kennet & Avon Canal was opened, boats were able to travel on from Newbury to Devizes, Bath and Bristol. During the nineteenth century the Kennet & Avon suffered from railway competition (the Great Western Railway virtually duplicated its route) and its decline continued until through trading ceased during the 1930s. By 1950 the canal was virtually unnavigable, and is only now being reopened section by section because of an immense effort by voluntary labour. Eventually craft should be able once again to navigate through from Reading to Bristol; at the time of writing it is possible to take a boat about ten miles up the Kennet from Reading.

One of the last watermen to trade on the Kennet & Avon was Ted Wilkins of Reading, who with his horsedrawn barge *Phoebe* would sometimes work through to Bristol. His daughter Mrs Boyd is landlady of the Thames Tavern by Blake's lock, and she recalls childhood trips on the barge, which also used to trade regularly on the Thames above and below Reading. *Phoebe* was a broad-beam boat, a true barge, not to be confused with a canal narrow boat with a beam of only seven feet.

In his last years Ted Wilkins would walk down the towpath from Reading to Sonning Mill, where he would help to load and unload the barges which still came there. Now the mill is closed and silent, and there are plans to turn it into a restaurant, although Sonning already has three eating-places. The parish is peculiar in that it extends on to both banks of the Thames, and is therefore both in Oxfordshire and in Berkshire; it is united by a handsome old eleven-arched bridge.

Gate from the towpath to the French Horn Hotel, Sonning.

Sonning Lock is a little above the bridge. The keeper here in the mid-nineteenth century was James Sadler, parish clerk, bee keeper, and poet, who wrote of his village:

> Is there a spot more lovely than the rest,
> By art improved, by nature truly blest?
> A noble river at its base is running,
> It is a little village known as Sonning.

Which at least clears up the matter of how the village's name should be pronounced.

The Thames runs through open country now, and soon the St Patrick's Stream leads off to the right, carrying Thames water out of the river and returning it lower down; once it brought the waters of the Loddon *into* the Thames, but the flow changed direction when the height of a weir at Shiplake was raised.

If you are walking, you will now have to make your first detour since Reading, as the towpath is interrupted below Shiplake Lock. It has always had to change sides here, originally for the sake of just one house with land running down to the water on the Shiplake bank, and Lashbrook and Bolney Ferries were within a ridiculously short distance of each other. Today the ferries have gone, and you must walk through Shiplake village and down a prosperous road, for that one house has multiplied into dozens of affluent villas with curious names. A footpath leads back to the river, and so to Marsh Lock, which is oddly situated in the middle of the stream and is reached by a long wooden causeway that carries the towpath. A short mile then leads you to Henley.

### HENLEY ROYAL REGATTA

Just downstream of Henley Bridge the course of the river is, for a little over a mile and a quarter, unobstructed and remarkably straight. This stretch, between the bridge and Temple Island, is Henley Reach: the scene every first week in July of Henley Royal Regatta, and the hub of the rowing world.

The Regatta had its formal beginning at a public meeting in Henley Town Hall on 26 March 1839, and therefore claims to be one of the oldest river regattas in the world. The account of that meeting records a resolution 'That from the lively interest which has been manifested at the various boat races which have taken place on the Henley Reach during the last few years, and the great influx of visitors on such occasions, this meeting is of the opinion that the establishing of an annual regatta, under a judicious and respectable management, would not only be productive of the most beneficial results to the town of Henley, but from its peculiar attractions would also be a source

An early picture of Henley Royal Regatta.

of amusement and gratification to the neighbourhood, and to the public in general.' In 1851 Prince Albert gave the event his patronage, and so made it the Henley Royal Regatta.

To a rowing man the names of the oldest prizes have a peculiar magic: the Grand Challenge Cup, for eight-oared boats, awarded since the first year of the Regatta; the Ladies' Challenge Plate, for eights from schools or colleges; the Wyfold, the Visitors' and the Stewards' Challenge Cups, for fours; the Silver Goblets for pairs, and the Diamond Sculls for the single sculler. These all date from the 1840s. There have been additions to the time-table of races since then, such a double-sculling race, one for coxed fours, and the Princess Elizabeth Challenge Cup, instituted in 1946 for public schools in the United Kingdom, and opened in 1964 to entries from schools overseas.

Since 1966 all the first class events have been open to crews from abroad, but the Regatta became cosmopolitan long before that. The first trophy to go abroad was the Diamond Sculls, won by a Dutchman in 1892. A Harvard crew won the Grand Challenge Cup in 1914, and in 1964 the men who had made up that crew presented a replica to replace the then ageing and fragile original trophy. American schools and colleges won the Thames Challenge Cup no less than seventeen times in the nineteen Regattas between 1936 and

Spectators at Henley, past and present.

A gondola among a flotilla of small craft at Henley, circa 1890 (*Henry Taunt*).

1960 and, among the other nationalities competing, Russian and German crews have been notably successful.

The accents of Henley competitors have grown more disparate in another way, too, in comparatively recent years. The Regatta began as an event for 'gentlemen amateurs'. It is still amateur, but the interpretation of the word 'gentleman' has been less exclusive since shortly after the First World War, when a row involving an 'artisan' rower, Jack Kelly, led to the rules being changed to allow manual workers to compete. There was an unforeseen reward for that magnanimity; Jack Kelly's grandaughter is now Princess Grace of Monaco and an active supporter of the Regatta. The definition of 'amateur', however, remains rigid. It excludes any who have received money for rowing or its supporting activities: coaching, boatbuilding or the work of college or club waterman. The famous sculler Ken Dwan is a Thames Lighterman and a regular competitor at Henley who before 1920 would have been doubly disqualified, both for his manual work and for having won a cash prize in the 'professional' Doggett's Coat and Badge Race. With the removal of one barrier between the 'gentlemen' and the 'artisans' the incentives to remove the others were strong. The Doggett prize is now a trophy, and 'professional' and wager races have died out on the river.

Nevertheless the Regatta still seems to suffer the appearance of being more exclusive than it is, for another historical reason. The management of the event is in the hands of forty 'Stewards'. To be elected one of the Henley Stewards is perhaps the most coveted responsibility in the English-speaking rowing world. In this constellation of eminent old rowing men are representatives of the Privy Council, the peerage, the armed services and the bench of bishops, and in 1974 an American, Hart Perry of Kent School, became the first non-Commonwealth Steward. From these men are chosen the year's committee of management, the umpires, judges, and timekeepers, and their name is given to the Stewards' Enclosure, the sanctum during Regatta Week to which admission is most closely guarded. Ties or cravats must be worn. But it is in fact more the pedigree than the present rules of the Stewards' Enclosure that is to blame for its forbidding reputation. Originally each of the most exclusive London clubs, White's, Boodle's, the Carlton and the rest, had its own small enclosure and tent at the Regatta, as did each of the rowing clubs. After the First World War, for economy's sake, the enclosures were amalgamated into one, and its original members were those members of the gentlemen's clubs. But since then membership has widened, naturally and by the deliberation of the organisers. To join the Stewards' enclosure a man must be proposed and seconded by two existing members (so that he may be trusted to pay his refreshment bill), but the organisers see the Enclosure now as having simply the function of a football supporters' club.

Certainly its subscriptions, and the additional fees that members pay for visitor's badges, are the greatest single source of the Regatta's income. (£65,000 came from this direction in 1974.) To it is added the gate money from the public or 'Regatta' enclosure, and the revenue from any out-of-season use of the Regatta's own 160 acres of riverside land. But in 1974 Henley Week cost nearly £100,000, a sum made up mainly of hire charges for tents and stands, with lesser but still huge sums spent on piling and booms to mark the course, and on ordinary maintenance of the river bank. The Regatta pays corporation tax, and receives no grant. In 1974 the final surplus of income over expenditure was £500.

According to Mr John Garton, the present Chairman of the Regatta, the margin between profit and loss is regularly very small; the event can just keep its head above water financially if the weather is not too bad. With the Regatta in this precarious state, the organisers have searched for a cure. It was felt that charges for members and other spectators had already been raised as much as they could be, and that only some new fund-raising idea could give the Regatta a secure future.

The first such idea was to develop some of the Regatta land. But a proposal to build twenty or thirty houses and a marina on Fawley Meadow near the Marlow road was vehemently opposed by Henley residents, and was dropped, despite the fact (remarks John Garton) that the town appears to tolerate more blatant eyesores.

The next attempt at a solution was to institute, in 1974, the experiment of Sunday racing. Saturday at Henley has long been regarded as a red-letter day in the English social calendar, ranking for many people second only to Royal Ascot. Serious rowing men decry the fashionable aspects of the Regatta, and speak tartly of those who come not to look at the crews but at each other. Nevertheless the organisers know that the event's survival depends on drawing a good crowd, of whatever motive. It was hoped that to shift the climax of the Regatta to Sunday would bring in the profitable crowds not just on one, but on two of the four racing days. The first year was disappointing, but the experiment continues.

Linked to Sunday racing has been another modification of the Henley tradition. Over the last few years the Regatta has found itself, or at any rate its races for schools, seriously threatened by a set of examinations: those set by the Oxford and Cambridge Joint Board, who happened to arrange papers on the dates of the Regatta. Not all schools sat those particular examinations, but there were enough good school crews suddenly found missing from the main events to make the organisers fear both for the standard of the races and for the lost revenue from the boys' parents. Their answer was the 'Special Race for Schools' rowed since 1974, with its shortened course, entry limited to those taking examinations, and heats on Saturday and Sunday only.

Another solution to the problem of the Regatta finances may prove to be the Henley Boat Festival, with demonstrations of craft by boatbuilders, waterborne concerts, fashion shows, and a grand ball under royal patronage. If this festival becomes an established event in the calendar of the boating world, as the Regatta organisers hope it will, the revenue from it may provide a watertight financial future for the Regatta itself, making profitable use of the Regatta land and river-frontage outside Henley Week.

AN ALTERED COURSE

Out of season the Regatta leaves few visible traces, yet it has left a permanent mark on the outline of the river itself.

The original rowing course at Henley began at the upstream end of Temple Island, turned a comparatively sharp corner at Poplar Point not far from the finish, and ended rather nearer the bridge than it now does. This course gave boats on the Berkshire side a potential advantage, though this was frequently cancelled by the buffeting of the wind, for the Buckinghamshire side was more sheltered. To add to the competitors' difficulties, there seems to have been little attempt in the early days to keep spectators' boats out of the way, and crews had to thread a path through an obstacle-course of picnic parties.

The course (though not the discipline of spectators) was greatly improved in 1886 when the finishing line was moved to Poplar Point, to avoid the bend there, while the start was moved correspondingly downstream. This course, which was in use until 1922, had only two slight angles. At the same time the number of crews taking part in any one heat was limited to two, and eventually the confusion of spectators' boats was cured by marking the course with a clear boundary of booms. But the ideal of a truly straight course still tantalised the Regatta. In 1923 an Experimental Course, straight but slightly shorter, was tried out; times achieved that year do not count in the official records. The next year began the era of the present Straight Course, which was only achieved by excavating parts of Temple Island and the Berkshire bank, but is the traditional and original length of 1 mile 550 yards. It is eighty feet wide and ends at Poplar Point.

A much more radical change in the Henley course was once mooted by John Garton, who besides being Regatta Chairman is President of the Amateur Rowing Association. He suggested modernising the event to conform to the ARA and international pattern, which would mean widening the river to allow *repêchage* or multi-lane rowing. But nobody in the world, he discovered, wanted Henley changed, and the Regatta remains the odd one out among international rowing events. Crews new to Henley have sometimes been caught out, unprepared and untrained for its length. But in other countries there are now 'imitation Henleys' complete with marks to represent its salient features, so that oarsmen may train for this unique course.

In another way, however, Henley has come up to date. Women were admitted as coxes at the 1975 Regatta for the first time, an arrangement already customary at other amateur rowing events. The more revolutionary idea that women should actually *row* at Henley is still as remote a possibility as ever; for the time being the organisers believe that the practical difficulties of providing changing facilities for two sexes in a tented camp can resist any feminist arguments.

One tradition persists at Henley that draws to the Regatta a group of men who neither row nor 'support'. For many years a week's duty at Henley Regatta has been one of the 'perks' which can come the way of an Oxford college servant or 'scout', and to be one of the Oxford scouts at Henley is thought of as having a paid holiday. The scouts are recognizable by their uniform of sober suit and tie, and straw boater with black band. As well as discreetly policing the entrances to the various enclosures, they supervise the embarkation of the few passengers allowed to follow each race in the umpire's launch, and guard propriety of behaviour and dress. The job is popular, with a waiting list of applicants, and many of the Oxford scouts are old and familiar faces at the Regatta, coming every year that their college can spare them.

The college scouts are all that remain of what, until the last war, used to

Oxford 'scouts' at Henley.

be an annual pilgrimage to Henley in search of work, and which brought, among others, all the boat hire firms from between Oxford and London. Henley Regatta was considered to be an event at which a lucky firm could really make money, and competition was fierce.

Each firm with pleasure boats for hire would, a fortnight before the start of the Regatta, be represented at an auction in Henley for a plot of ground on which to set up in business. The plots began about two hundred yards upstream of Henley Bridge and stretched for half a mile or more along Mill Meadows, and bidding was fierce for the most advantageous site. Then each firm would set up its sign and tent and bring in its stock of skiffs and punts.

George Harris of Oxford remembers being allowed to leave school to help his father make the two and a half day trip to Henley. Twenty-four punts at a time would be loaded, two abreast and four or five high, onto a narrow, horse-drawn 'monkey boat', and the staff would sleep each night on the way in the end of one of the stacked punts.

As soon as the boat firms were set up, there arrived on the scene a dozen or so professional touts, temporarily deserting the racecourses to barter their services for the highest commission the boatmen would offer. Then as the trains came in to Henley station the touts would be there to meet them, open the doors, and entrap customers for the boats. Yet, for all the brashness of their methods, the touts are remembered with affection by the watermen who knew them. They were colourful and talkative characters, and gave the

Regatta a certain spice, for the lack of which no amount of rowing men can compensate.

## SCANDAL AT THE WATER'S EDGE

The principal boat business in Henley is that of Hobbs & Son, founded in 1870. The firm is closely associated with the Regatta, and since 1919 has undertaken the special piling which marks the course. The job starts about Easter, builds up to a peak before the Regatta in July, and carries on until August as all the piles are removed again. Hobbs's men are said to know their job so well that the piles go back into last year's holes in the river-bed. The firm built and looks after three of the umpire's launches used at the Regatta, *Amaryllis, Enchantress* and *Magician*; these are also used at other regattas up and down the river such as Kingston, Staines, Moulsford, Maidenhead, Reading and Marlow and when not doing regatta work are used for public trips and hired out for private parties.

The Leander club stands on the Remenham bank near Henley bridge, and is frequented throughout the year by rowing men, who come to train, eat and drink. That unique colour 'Leander Pink' can be seen on many of the fittings. Some of the members' cars have stickers saying *The Leander Squad, supported by Pimm's,* and certainly a good deal of Pimm's cup and other liquor gets consumed in Henley at regatta time. Even in the winter you can see the occasional empty gin bottle floating in the reeds.

The striking little temple on Temple Island was built by Wyatt, the 'improver' of Fawley Court, and is not purely ornamental, for the back part is an inhabited cottage.

Not far downstream is Hambleden Lock, where Caleb Gould was keeper from 1777 until his death in 1836. He wore a long coat with many buttons, and ate a dish of onion porridge every night for his supper. Each day he walked into Hambleden, and made a cross on the ground to show how far he had been. He is buried in Remenham churchyard.

Hambleden Mill was working until 1958, and for the last twenty years of its life was powered by a water-driven turbine that replaced the earlier wheel, and is still in position in the mill-race, though now covered over and lying idle.

Below Culham Court, some maps mark 'Fish Weir' by the right bank. This refers to a set of eel traps or 'bucks' which were still in position here after the First World War, but have now disappeared. Another fish weir was once situated at Medmenham, where it was given the peculiar name of 'Poison Ducks', apparently from the Anglo-Norman *poisson duct* or fish weir. The fishing rights on the stretch of river between Hambleden and Medmenham

Eel traps on the Thames in the nineteenth century.

are let to the delightfully named Wimbledon Piscatorial Society.

On the north bank just before Medmenham Abbey is a monument erected to the memory of a court case: 'This Monument (reads the inscription) was erected to commemorate the successful action fought by Hudson Ewebank Kearley, First Viscount Devonport, which resulted in the Court of Appeal deciding on the 28th March 1899 that Medmenham Ferry is public.' The case arose because it was disputed whether or not the ferry that was operated at the Ferry Hotel, Medmenham, was an ancient public ferry (as Kearley, a local landowner, held it to be). The innkeeper worked the ferry, and was demanding a toll that was thought by some people to be unreasonable. The action (involving two pleas) was complex and probably expensive; after winning his case, Kearley erected the monument, presumably to ensure that no one ever forgot the outcome. Ironically, though, the monument remains the ferry has gone.

And so we come to the curious Gothic apparition of Medmenham Abbey, a place more associated with scandal than with saintliness, and linked in particular with the name of Sir Francis Dashwood. This eccentric nobleman was born in 1708, and when he was sixteen succeeded to his father's estates. He immediately became a pleasure seeker, was elected to the Beefsteak and Hellfire Clubs, became a 'Blood', and made a Grand Tour of Europe and Russia, during which (it was said) he was hardly ever sober. On his return he helped found the Dilettanti Society, which Horace Walpole described as 'a club for which the nominal qualification is having been to Italy, and the real one, being drunk'. He was elected as M.P. for New Romney in 1741, but continued his licentious course. In about 1745 he founded 'The Franciscans

Medmenham Abbey.

of Medmenham', taking their title from his Christian name; they were also known as 'The Knights of St Francis of Wycombe' (the family seat being at West Wycombe). Medmenham was the scene of their principal activities; there they rented and restored the old Cistercian abbey, and fixed over the entrance the Rabelaisian inscription 'Fay ce que voudras' (Do whatever you like). The 'Franciscans', who included the Prince of Wales and several earls, and for a short time the notorious John Wilkes, amused themselves with obscene parodies of the rites of the Roman Church. Dashwood acted as Grand-master, using a Communion chalice to pour out libations to heathen deities, and administering the Sacrament to a baboon.

Thanks to his influential friends, Dashwood became Chancellor of the Exchequer in 1762. But his budget speech was so confused and incompetent that it was received with shouts of derision, and he soon resigned. Eventually he became quite respectable, and died at West Wycombe in 1781; but although he was married he left no legitimate heirs. The sacrilegious decorations at the abbey were expunged, it resumed its former respectable character, and today it houses RAF Signals Command.

A relic of a very different kind stands on the north bank just above Hurley Lock: the last surviving weir-winch, one of many that were used to haul boats up the flash weirs. Immediately below it lies Harleyford Manor, once a quietly elegant country mansion (built in 1755) but now the site of a combined marina and caravan park. The seemingly endless line of moored boats here eventually concludes just short of Temple Lock, and soon the traveller reaches Marlow.

The suspension bridge at Marlow was opened in 1835, although there was

Weir-winch at Hurley.

a bridge here for at least 600 years before that. Recently another bridge has been added downstream of the town, carrying a link between two motorways. After that, the next crossing is at Bourne End, where a railway bridge carries a branch line towards Maidenhead. Here you will find the 'Upper Thames Sailing Club', which poses the question: where does the Upper Thames begin (or end)?

The next road and foot crossing is at Cookham, whose bridge was built in the latter part of the nineteenth century. And just below Cookham Lock is Cliveden.

The handsome Cliveden estate (overlooking one of the finest steeply wooded reaches of the Thames) has more than once provided the setting for sensational events. In 1668 its first owner, George Villiers, the dissolute Duke of Buckingham, killed the Earl of Shrewsbury in a duel fought on the terrace over Lady Shrewsbury, who was watching from the sidelines disguised as a page, and cheered her victorious lover. It was at a Cliveden masque in 1740 that 'Rule Britannia' was first performed, with the composer, Dr Arne, conducting. The house itself was burned down three times, once because a chambermaid had been reading in bed by candlelight. After the fire of 1849 Sir Charles Barry, the architect of the Houses of Parliament, designed the present sumptuous Italianate mansion, which has forty-six bedrooms.

An American hotel proprietor, William Waldorf Astor, bought it from the Duke of Westminster in 1893 for $6,000,000, and later became the first Lord Astor. His son, the second Viscount, who owned the *Observer* newspaper (another branch of the family were proprietors of *The Times*) was given the

Cliveden and the riverside cottage.

house as a wedding present. He and his wife held weekend house-parties whose guests were in 1936 dubbed 'the Cliveden Set'; Claud Cockburn coined the phrase when he accused the Astors and their influential friends of plotting appeasement with Nazi Germany. (Lord Astor's American-born wife Nancy, the first woman Member of Parliament, dismissed the story as 'astonishin' rubbish'.) And the house was later to feature again, with more startling results, in the fortunes of the Conservative party.

In 1942 the Astors handed over Cliveden to the National trust, but stayed there to live in their accustomed style, the house being open to the public generally on one day a week. The third Lord Astor, William Waldorf, succeeded to the title in 1952, and in the years that followed he entertained at Cliveden on a scale at least equalling if not exceeding in splendour what had gone before. The gossip columns carried frequent accounts of midnight fireworks, champagne on the terraces, and royalty mingling with film stars. Ascot Week was the climax of the Cliveden social calendar.

There was also the cottage in the grounds, the ornate little house on the left bank just below Formosa Island, near the site of My Lady Ferry (the last ferry to be operated by the Thames Conservancy). This cottage was rented by Stephen Ward, who as an osteopath and portrait painter was patronised by many celebrated people, including members of the Royal Family. Lord Astor rented the cottage to Ward for one pound a year, and here Ward entertained his friends, among them the model and showgirl Christine Keeler. In the summer of 1961, Mr John Profumo, Secretary of State for War, encountered Miss Keeler by chance at Cliveden, and what followed is well known: the rumours, Profumo's eventual resignation, and a scandal which at one time seemed to involve almost every eminent person in Britain, and which rocked the Conservative government of the time.

Gradually the Profumo affair was relegated to the history books. The third Lord Astor died in 1966, and the house at Cliveden was given up by the family. In May of that year the contents of the mansion were auctioned in 2,067 lots, which included seed-pearls, suitcases, huck-a-back face towels, hemstitched pillow-cases, a sedan chair and a banjo. Cliveden's era of glory was over.

Yet the breath of scandal still hangs around the Thames in these parts. In 1974 Lieutenant Colonel John Brookes, then aged sixty-four and formerly Mayor of Kensington and Chelsea, sued the *Sunday People*; that newspaper had published an article describing how a nineteen-year-old girl had answered his advertisement for 'good-natured young ladies' to crew his motor yacht on the Thames. The girl was taken to the boat, which was moored at Maidenhead, and after removing her clothes, she had her bottom spanked by Colonel Brookes, who then poured whiskey on it 'to relieve the pain'. The Colonel won his libel action, but was only awarded ½p damages.

HER MAJESTY'S SWANS

An old-fashioned weatherboarded boathouse at Cookham houses the offices of Turk & Sons, where Mr John Turk presides over the boat hire and repair business. It is also his duty to organize the annual Swan Upping, for he is Swan Keeper to Her Majesty the Queen.

He was appointed to the job in 1963 when his father Frederick Turk retired after forty-one years' service. He says that the handling of the birds is learnt from experience. They can be ferocious when they are guarding their nests, eggs, and young, and could indeed break an arm (or more likely a wrist) as they are popularly supposed to be able to do. But mostly he handles the swans when they are injured, and then they are comparatively docile. The birds hurt themselves when they fly into overhead power cables or land on a road when it is shimmering in the summer heat, thinking it to be a river.

The first mention of the post of Royal Swan Keeper dates from 1295, but the job is probably older than that. The swan has long been regarded as a royal bird (though Mr Turk discounts the legend that the first swan was brought to England from Cyprus by Richard Coeur de Lion). Anciently, and until recent times, the swan was a game bird, eaten at table and much in demand; hence the collective plural 'a game of swans'. The swan only disappeared from the kitchen when the turkey was imported into Britain. The privilege of owning swans has always been granted by the Crown; in

Swan Upping in Victorian times.

previous centuries many of the nobility living near the river owned a game, although chief among owners have always been the rich livery companies of the City of London. Nowadays there are only three owners: the Vintners' Company, the Dyers' Company, and Her Majesty the Queen.

A distinguishing mark has always been used to establish ownership of the birds. Swan owners in the Fens would cut designs in the webs of the bird's feet, but on the Thames the marks have always been made by cutting notches in the upper beak or mandible, and stopping the slight bleeding with pitch. With only three owners, the modern system of marking is simple: Royal birds are unmarked; those belonging to the Vintners have a notch on each side of the mandible; while those belonging to the Dyers have a notch on one side only. (The rings that many swans have on their legs are put there by ornithologists conducting a census.)

The marking is done at the annual Swan Upping (or Hopping as it was sometimes called). This is done in the season when the cygnets are old enough to be handled, for it is they rather than the adult birds who have to be picked up and dealt with. The third week in July is the regular time for the event.

John Turk organises the Upping. The other people principally involved are his cousin Mr Michael Turk (from the Kingston branch of the family), who is the Vintners' Company Swan Master, and Mr H. E. Cobb who is Swan Keeper to the Dyers' Company. They are assisted by a number of licensed watermen from further down the river (principally from the tideway) who row the boats and physically handle the swans. The boats are mostly

John Turk, Her Majesty's Swan Keeper.

double-sculling skiffs, but John Turk himself travels in his randan, a rare survival of a once popular type of boat, which is rowed by three men, two with single oars and one with a pair of sculls.

The Crown owns about 500 swans and cygnets between Blackfriars and Henley, the upper limit of the Swan Keeper's jurisdiction. In addition, the Dyers are allocated sixty-five birds and the Vintners forty-five. Although swans are no longer required for City and Royal banquets, the cygnets are still allocated and marked where necessary. Where swans have inter-mated with birds belonging to other owners, their cygnets are allocated between the owners of the parents (the owner of the male bird getting first choice). Members of the 'courts' of the Dyers' and Vintners' Companies come to watch and sport, and members of the Royal Family are often there too. After the day's work, the watermen and Swan Keepers retire to the pub, where, according to one observer, 'you need hollow legs to keep up with the amount of beer they drink'.

128

Royal barges: these modern replicas were built for the film *A Man For All Seasons*. King Henry VIII, played by Robert Shaw, travels in the nearer his musicians in the further barge (*Trevor Ryland*).

### ROYALTY ON THE RIVER

Maidenhead Railway Bridge, forming two elegant spans across the Thames, is one of the triumphs of the architect of the Great Western Railway, Isambard Kingdom Brunel. Despite doubts expressed by critics at the time of its erection as to whether the 'insignificant little bricks' of which its arches are formed could carry the trains, the bridge (widened since its original construction) is sound and in service nearly a century and a half later. The next bridge, which crosses the river a mile and a half below Maidenhead, contrasts strongly in style of construction and function; it carries the M4 motorway and was built in 1961.

Accompanied by the drone of motorway traffic and the whine of jets from the nearby Heathrow Airport, we progress past the faded eighteenth century glories of Monkey Island and Down Place at Bray; the former now houses an hotel, the latter a film studio with a prolific output of horror films. Perhaps the proprietors chose the site with an eye on Oakley Court, the neighbouring mansion, which is a veritable Dracula's Castle of mid-Victoriana.

Already Windsor Castle is making tantalising appearances over the tree tops, and after a few desultory meanders at Boveney and Clewer, the Thames is soon flowing past the castle walls and under Eton bridge.

The castle dates from the twelfth century, but of all monarchs who have lived there, Victoria left the greatest imprint on it, and her spirit and statue still preside over the town. A magnificent railway station built by the G.W.R. does homage to the castle opposite, although the platforms formerly used for royal arrivals and departures now serve as a car park.

Left to right: the Queen's Bargemaster, Bert Barry, with Royal Watermen Charles Taylor, Frank Dott, and George Saunders (*Keystone Press Agency*).

Long before the first royal train rolled out of Windsor station, the monarch and his (or her) consort would often travel as a matter of course by water between the royal palaces that stood on the banks of the Thames. For example: King John had wine and provisions brought to him at Windsor by water; Edward II hired boats to send his son and his knights and clerks from Windsor to the Tower of London; Henry VIII usually travelled by boat from Windsor to the capital. Elizabeth I made great use of the river, particularly in London. In 1557 she was anxious to encourage the hopes of her suitor Charles, son of the Holy Roman Emperor. She met his Ambassador rowing on the Thames, offered him a seat in the Treasurer's boat, laid her own barge alongside, and talked to him and played on the lute. Two days later she invited him out in her own boat and made him take the helm. And even today, Queen Elizabeth II occasionally makes a journey along the river. In October 1974 she toured the Royal Borough of Windsor and Maidenhead partly by launch, embarking at Hurley Lock and disembarking at Magna Carta Island, where she planted a walnut tree to mark the occasion.

Present on that day were the Queen's Bargemaster and a number of Royal Watermen. There are two dozen of the latter (there used to be fifty) and up to the beginning of the present century their principal duty was to row the

Prince Frederick's Barge, built in 1731-2 (*National Maritime Museum*).

State Barge, a large rowing-boat with a canopied seat for the monarch and consort. Generally ten rowers were required, and the Bargemaster would steer. The last State Barge to be used in England was known as Queen Mary's Shallop, and it has had a long and active life. It was built by William III for Mary the Queen in 1689, and from 1849 it was the only remaining State Barge of the English Crown. It was still in service in 1912, when it carried George V and his Queen Mary at Henley Royal Regatta, and its last water-borne appearance was on the tideway at London in August 1919 when the King and Queen attended a Peace Pageant. In 1930 George V presented it to the National Maritime Museum at Greenwich, where it can be seen along-side the lavishly decorated Prince Frederick's Barge.

But though the State Barge is laid up, the Royal Watermen are still required to be in attendance when the monarch makes a journey by river. A number of them also ride on the back of the royal coach at the State opening of Parliament, a relic of the days when that journey was made by water from the Tower of London. To be a Royal Waterman is a highly sought-after honour on the Thames; among present holders of the office are John Turk of Cookham, Michael Turk of Kingston, and Charles Taylor, Bargemaster to the Fishmongers' Company (see Chapter 8). The Queen's Bargemaster is Bert Barry, also a professional waterman.

JOLLY BOATING WEATHER

Eton College, standing a little way back from the river on the opposite bank to Windsor, in the middle of Eton town, is intimately associated with the Thames. The college was founded by Henry VI in 1440 (some of its buildings date from the foundation), and from the earliest days a strict routine was imposed on pupils that left little time for the enjoyment of the river. However,

Eton boys at Romney Lock, circa 1880. A sail is being hoisted on the skiff.

swimming seems to have been a common pastime for pupils from the beginning. Accidents were frequent, and there was a superstition even as late as the 1880s that a boy would be drowned every third year.

Rowing at Eton seems to have begun late in the eighteenth century, and there were organised regattas by 1793. The town became well supplied with boathouses and boatbuilders, so that a boy like Percy Bysshe Shelley (who was at Eton in the early 1800s) could escape the rigours of school and row off by himself to a quiet reach of the river. Early in the nineteenth century a river entertainment was incorporated into the 'Fourth of June', the school's celebration in honour of George III's birthday, and there were boating events on 'Election Saturday'. For some years there was also an annual trip up the river for a supper provided by a local dignitary at Surly Hall, Boveney.

Races against Westminster School began in 1829, the year of the first Oxford and Cambridge Boat Race, and soon became a matter of tradition, despite some opposition from those who did not yet consider rowing to be a safe and tolerable occupation for schoolboys. The boats used at the College ranged from the little 'funnies' for one sculler, through fours, sixes and eights, to the magnificent ten-oared *Monarch*.

Thomas Kynaston Selwyn, who was a pupil at Eton in the late 1820s, wrote an account in classical Greek of events on the river in his time; it includes a description of Keate, the Headmaster, tramping the river bank trying to catch boys who were disobeying his orders that no boats were to go out before Easter. But in the summer 'half' of 1830, boating was approved of,

132

especially at the Fourth of June celebrations. On these occasions it was customary for distinguished guests to be 'sitters' or passengers in the boats; in the evening the sitter would pay for a large dinner for the crew. At the Fourth in 1830, the sitter in *Monarch* was to have been George, son of the Duke of Cumberland, but he could not come because the King was ill, and instead sent a message (as Selwyn records) that 'he would give as many bottles of wine as the crew of *Monarch* asked for, and they asked for six dozen, and these were given . . . On June 19th the first Duck-and-Green-Pea night was held . . . The Boats were in full gala dress, for they did not use the ordinary rudders, but snakes and flags, as on the great days . . . The wine at Surly Hall was partly that left from the six dozen given by George.' King George IV died on 26 June, but that did not stop the Lower Boats' Dinner, at which 'some drank too much, and were flogged the next morning'.

Eton College took part at Henley Royal Regatta for the first time in 1861, and in 1864 won the Ladies' Plate, thus beginning a long if not always consistent record of successes at the Regatta. Eton's fame as a rowing school has, perhaps, also been increased by its Boating Song, not often sung at the school today, but still remembered by many Old Etonians:

> Jolly boating weather,
> And a hay harvest breeze;
> Blade on the feather,
> Shade on the trees.
> Swing, swing together,
> With your bodies between your knees,
> Swing, swing together,
> With your bodies between your knees.

### MR BOLLAND OF WRAYSBURY

There is yet another detour for the towpath walker below Eton, for the path runs for a mile and a half through Windsor Home Park, and Royalty does not permit the public to use it for walking, though reputedly there is an actual right of towing from the path.

If you are not towing a boat, and are on foot, you must leave the river at Victoria Bridge, and go through Datchet, rejoining the towpath below that village at Albert Bridge. The two bridges (which replaced an earlier one in Datchet itself) are supposed to have been designed by Prince Albert himself.

Now the river takes us first to Old Windsor, where there was a Saxon palace, and then to Wraysbury on the opposite bank. Here lives a man with a unique collection of books and pictures about the Thames.

If you are an observant reader of Thames guidebooks, you will have seen the name R. R. Bolland, found under many of the photographs. Reginald Bolland worked for the Thames Conservancy from 1932 until 1973, and was involved in the administration of the navigation department. But his interest in the river soon spread beyond his working hours, and in the 1950s he began to collect books on the Thames, particularly the great nineteenth century tomes full of elegant plates. He also began to build up a library of photographs of the river, mainly taken by himself, and soon extended his interest to nineteenth-century watercolours of Thames scenes.

Reg Bolland eventually reached a senior position in the Thames Conservancy: among his responsibilities was the organisation of the annual inspection of the river by the Conservators. But in 1973 he left the Conservancy, choosing early retirement before the 'take-over' by the new Thames Water Authority. He says he is pessimistic about the future of the river under the new management; he dislikes the constant emphasis on the coming water shortage, which he says is 'to keep the planners in a job'. He is also concerned about the failure of local authorities to exercise proper control over moorings and the construction of new marinas.

He is now devoting much of his time to writing; in 1975 his book *Victorians on the Thames* was published, and he has other projects under way. He is also involved with the administration of the River Thames Society. And from his study window he watches the river, a few yards away, through its changing seasons.

WATER FOR THE CARDINAL

Almost opposite Reg Bolland's window is Runnymede, where Magna Carta was signed in 1215; the barons chose the place because it was conveniently near their own camp at Staines, and not too far from King John's castle at Windsor. Runnymede now houses the memorial to President Kennedy, which is situated on an acre of ground given to the American people.

A mile downstream on the left bank stands the London Stone, marking the limit of the City of London's active jurisdiction over the river until the mid-nineteenth century. When the Lord Mayor and Aldermen of the City visited the Stone in their shallop or row-barge, there was a custom of bumping the Sheriffs and Aldermen who had not been made 'Free of the Waters'. Toasts were drunk and small coins thrown to the crowd, and the Lord Mayor's name would be inscribed upon the Stone. In 1857 the Thames Conservators were granted control of the river from here downwards, and arranged for 'Thames Conservancy 1857' to be carved on the Stone, the last inscription to be made there.

The Thames flows through Laleham and Chertsey to Weybridge, where it reaches its southernmost point. The town was once an important junction, for the River Wey navigation formerly led to the Wey & Arun Canal, which in turn led to the River Arun and the South Coast. The canal has been closed for more than a hundred years, but there are faint hopes that this 'lost route to the sea' may one day be reopened. Meanwhile the Wey itself is still navigable for launches as far as Guildford and sometimes as far as Godalming.

Immediately downstream of Weybridge, the Thames makes a big meander (still navigable) to Shepperton, which is by-passed by the modern Desborough Cut, opened in 1935 and named after the Conservancy's most illustrious Chairman. With the aid of this short-cut, the navigator can in a relatively short time reach Walton-on-Thames, where the handsome nineteenth-century bridge is almost hidden by a steel structure alongside, carrying the traffic which is too heavy for the older bridge. Below Walton come the giant reservoirs of the old Metropolitan Water Board at Sunbury (where there are two locks side by side), and, on the left bank below Hampton, the great park and palace of Hampton Court.

Thomas Wolsey acquired the lease of the old manor of Hampton Court in 1514, and immediately began to erect a vast edifice there. He surrounded the house and garden with a great moat, and arranged for rain-water and sewage to be carried off into the Thames by brick sewers three feet wide and five feet high. The system proved so efficient that it was not superseded until 1871.

Wolsey also wanted to provide the purest water he possibly could for his household. The Thames was then comparatively clean, but it was not good enough for him. Instead he chose the springs at Coombe Hill, three and a half miles from the palace, on the opposite side of the river. There, several conduits collected the water, which was then conveyed by force of gravity in a double set of pipes from Coombe to Surbiton, under the Hogsmill River (a tributary of the Thames), under the Thames itself above Kingston Bridge, and so through the park to the palace. The pipes were each two and a half inches wide, were made of lead half an inch thick, and were laid down in twenty-five feet lengths. The total fall of 160 feet from Coombe Springs to the Palace must have provided excellent water-pressure. Apparently the water itself tasted good, but turned the vegetables black.

After Wolsey's fall and death, Henry VIII enlarged Hampton Court, and much later William and Mary (with Wren as architect) had it rebuilt so that the watercourse was mostly obliterated; but you can still see its line crossing the park from the semi-circular garden east of the palace.

Like the other royal palaces on the Thames, Hampton Court was often approached by the monarch in the royal barge. Some years ago, two full-size replicas of this type of barge were built by Bob Gibbs of Trowlock Island,

Obelisk below Teddington Lock, marking the end of the Thames Conservancy's and the beginning of the Port of London Authority's jurisdiction.

just below Kingston, for use in the film based on the life of Sir Thomas More, *A Man For All Seasons*. After the filming, the barges were kept at Turk's boat-house in Kingston; appropriately the pub next door to the boathouse is called The Row-Barge.

Below Trowlock Island you can hear the roaring of Teddington Weir, the lowest on the Thames. Although the derivation of the name Teddington as 'Tide End Town' is not generally accepted, there is a pub called the Tide End Cottage near Teddington Lock, and here, since the weir and lock were first built in 1811, the tide has been held back from the river above. There are three lock chambers: the Skiff Lock, which at 5ft 10ins by 49ft 6ins is probably the smallest lock in Britain; the Old Lock, measuring nearly 178ft by 24ft 4ins; and the Barge Lock, which at its full extent measures 650ft by 24ft 9ins, although it is generally used as a 'half lock' by shutting a pair of gates part of the way along it. A notice dated 1882 warns pleasure craft to give way to 'barges and steam vessels', but the former are almost as rare here now as the latter, and the lock staff deal for the most part with the pleasure traffic. Here is Tough's boatyard, capable of building and repairing the largest size of river-craft; and here you pass out of the relatively gentle current of the non-tidal river into the fierce and often unpredictable ebb and flow of the tideway. So it is best to ask the advice of the lock keepers, and to obtain the navigation instructions issued by the Port of London Authority, before going further downstream.

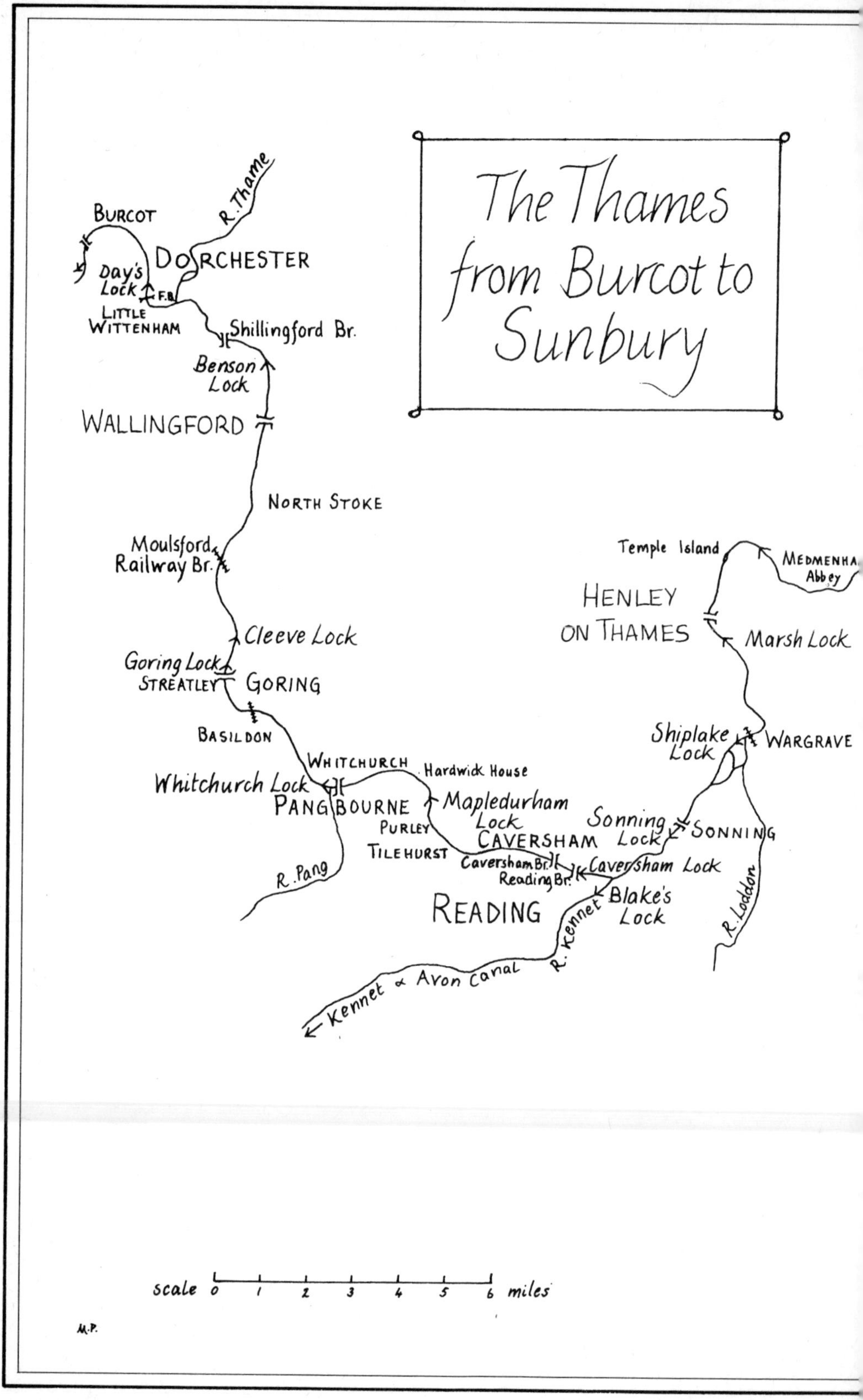

The Thames from Burcot to Sunbury

BURCOT
R. Thame
DORCHESTER
Day's Lock
F.B.
LITTLE WITTENHAM
Shillingford Br.
Benson Lock
WALLINGFORD
NORTH STOKE
Moulsford Railway Br.
Cleeve Lock
Goring Lock
STREATLEY GORING
BASILDON
WHITCHURCH
Hardwick House
Whitchurch Lock
PANGBOURNE
Mapledurham Lock
PURLEY
TILEHURST
CAVERSHAM
R. Pang
Caversham Br.
Reading Br.
Caversham Lock
READING
Blake's Lock
R. Kennet
Kennet & Avon Canal

Temple Island
MEDMENHAM Abbey
HENLEY ON THAMES
Marsh Lock
Shiplake Lock
WARGRAVE
Sonning Lock
SONNING
R. Loddon

scale 0 1 2 3 4 5 6 miles

M.P.

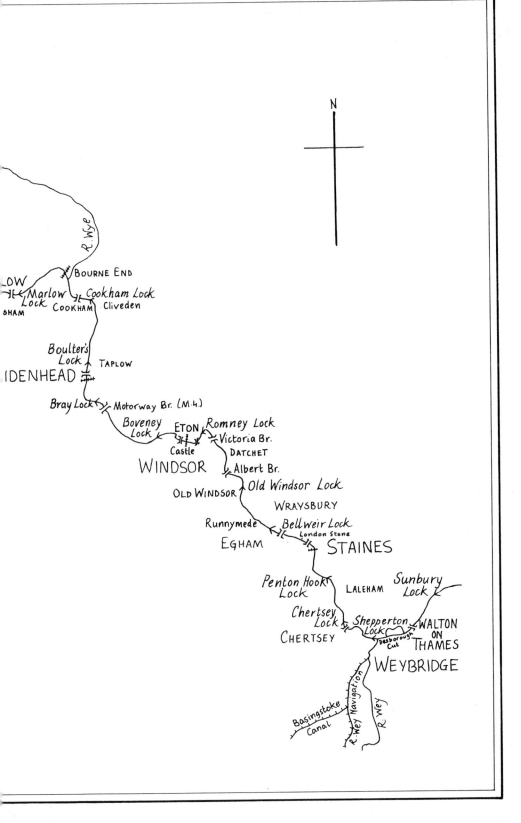

N

R. Wye

OW ___ BOURNE END
 ⊬ Marlow ⊬ Cookham Lock
  Lock  COOKHAM Cliveden
SHAM

Boulter's
Lock ⊬ TAPLOW
IDENHEAD ≢

Bray Lock ⊬ Motorway Br. (M.4.)
        Boveney     Romney Lock
         Lock  ETON ⊬ Victoria Br.
              Castle  DATCHET
WINDSOR ⊬ Albert Br.
     OLD WINDSOR ⊬ Old Windsor Lock
            WRAYSBURY
   Runnymede ⊬ Bellweir Lock
            London Stone
   EGHAM        STAINES

    Penton Hook  LALEHAM   Sunbury
      Lock                   Lock
   Chertsey          Shepperton    WALTON
     Lock           Lock  Desborough  ON
   CHERTSEY              Cut      THAMES
                         WEYBRIDGE

              Basingstoke
                Canal  R. Wey Navigation  R. Wey

# VIII

# The Tideway

Even if you do not notice the tide at first, you will realise that things are different when you get below Richmond. A lock and weir span the river here, but they are quite unlike anything above Teddington. The weir may be there when you arrive, or it may not. For some time either side of high water the gates are lifted and turned on their side by a heavy counterweighted mechanism, and then you can pass straight through under the footbridge. At other times the gates are lowered to help keep up the water level along the reach above; then you must pass through the lock and pay quite a considerable toll to the Port of London Authority.

Do not forget to notice the site of Richmond Palace when you pass it; only a gateway remains, although the area retains more than a trace of its former splendour.

Queen Elizabeth I died here in the early spring of 1603, and her body was taken by water to Whitehall Palace at night. When James I came to the throne he went by barge from Whitehall to the Tower to receive the keys. Soon afterwards he travelled by river to Greenwich, and inspected men-of-war and pinnaces anchored in the Thames, which were shortly to set off on an expedition to harass the Spaniards. A few days later there was a triumphal display of fireworks on the river; and when he was crowned in July, those who attended at Westminster came by water to avoid the plague that was then raging in London.

In the same year as James I's accession, Dr Whitgift the Archbishop of Canterbury was on his way to a meeting at the Bishop of London's palace at Fulham. He went there from Lambeth by barge, and refused to have the side-cloths down even though it was a bitterly cold day. He caught a chill, and eventually died from it.

These few events of 1603 perhaps give some idea of the enormous part that the Thames played in life at the time. Everyone in London used the river as a highway. Barges were owned by the king, noblemen, the Lord Mayor and City Companies of London, and by merchants and burgesses. Lower ranks

Thames Waterman, circa 1825.

and the common people hired small boats to ferry them across or along the river. London Bridge was the only bridge in London, so the population had to take to the boats and use the services of watermen.

It is perhaps important at this stage to make the distinction between the two categories of 'professionals' on the tideway, watermen and lightermen. The 1859 Act which provides for 'the better regulation of Watermen, Barge Owners and Others' states: 'The term "Lighterman" shall mean any person working or navigating for hire a lighter, barge, boat or other like craft.' ('Lighter' is a term virtually interchangeable with 'barge'; the latter word now seems to be in greater use.) The Act continues: 'The term "Waterman" shall mean any person navigating, rowing, or working for hire, a passenger boat.'

For many centuries the function of the waterman was akin to that of a taxi driver today. He carried passengers between convenient landing places, generally the public steps or stairs still a prominent feature of the river in London, and he provided the normal means of transport across and up and down the Thames, until bridge building and the development of public transport on land drove him into extinction. His usual craft, the Thames wherry, vanished with him, and today only a few specimens survive. The wherry was a type of rowing boat peculiarly suited to the waterman's needs. It was clinker built (that is, with overlapping planks), had a raking stem, hollow bow lines with a pronounced flare, and a broad rounded stern. It was wide at the centre and could carry at least eight passengers comfortably. Also characteristic was the ornamental wooden backrest on which the name of the craft was displayed. Wherries were easy to row; generally the waterman

The canopied boat on the right is a row-barge or shallop, of the type used by high-ranking travellers.

sculled on his own, though an apprentice might sometimes assist him. When the boat was beached, the raked stem could be brought on to dry land for the convenience of passengers, and when they moved aft, the shift of weight would lift the boat off the bottom, and the waterman could push the wherry afloat. Wherries were fast in the water; the Secretary to the Venetian Ambassador wrote in 1618: 'The wherries shoot along so lightly as to surprise everyone . . . They (the watermen) row like galley oarsmen, with extremely long oars, and are very dextrous at steering clear of each other.'

### THE WATER POET

Watermen were firmly established long before 1514, in which year an Act regulated their fares, but was largely ignored. In 1555 another Act appointed Rulers over the watermen, and thus created what was to become the Company of Watermen and Lightermen of the River Thames; the lightermen were included in 1700. (The Company's motto is 'At Commandment Of Our Superiors'.) Also in 1555 an apprenticeship was introduced, and extended in 1603 from one year to seven.

A notable waterman in the early days of the company was John Taylor, 'the Water Poet'. Born of humble parentage at Gloucester in 1580, Taylor was sent to the grammar school there, but getting 'mired' in his Latin was apprenticed to a London waterman. At the age of 16, press-ganged into the

Navy, he served under Essex at the siege of Cadiz, and at 'Flores in the Azores' the following year. He later retired from the services with a lame leg, and returned to the trade of Thames waterman.

But it was a difficult living. The Navy had 'pressed' many watermen like Taylor into service in Spain, the Low Countries, and Ireland, leaving only a few of them at home to carry on the river's passenger traffic. But when theatre companies began to establish themselves on Bankside (among them Shakespeare and his fellow actors at the Globe) there was a great demand by the public to be ferried across to attend the plays. Consequently young lads were taken on as watermen in large numbers. When employment at sea diminished in the early 1600s, thousands of watermen came back to find scant work; the players had moved to the Middlesex shore, and the young lads were now grown men with families to support. At this time there were said to be 40,000 watermen plying for hire between Windsor and Gravesend. John Taylor records a suit of the watermen petitioning that the players should be made to return to Bankside. (The players' retort was that you might as well ask to shift the Exchange.) There was also an additional threat to the watermen's business along the river from hackney carriages and sedan chairs, but the Watermen's Company succeeded in keeping these out of London for many years unless their journeys ended at least two miles from the river.

Finding that these hard times did not produce an adequate living, John Taylor turned to making money by writing occasional verses on commission, generally to celebrate births, marriages and deaths. He also undertook strange journeys for reward, collecting subscriptions for the descriptive verses he published on his return. These journeys included a sea voyage by wherry from London to York, which Taylor called 'A very Merrie Wherrie-Ferry Voyage', and a trip he made from London down the estuary to Queenborough in Kent on a Saturday evening, with a vintner, in a boat made of brown paper with stockfish tied to canes for oars. The boat nearly fell to pieces, but they got there (more dead than alive) on Monday morning.

By 1613 Taylor was sufficiently distinguished to be commissioned to arrange a water pageant to celebrate the marriage of Princess Elizabeth; while at the royal courts of Europe during his foreign travels he styled himself 'Queen's Majesty's Poet'. His verse (of which a little is quoted in Chapters 4 and 5) has often been branded as doggerel, but it is full of humour, and gives us a good deal of useful information about contemporary conditions.

During the plague epidemic of 1625 Taylor lodged at Oriel College, Oxford, and returned there during the Civil War. At Oxford he was much esteemed for his 'facetious company'. His portrait hangs in the Bodleian Library. After the Civil War he took the Crown public house in Long Acre (now the Ship, Hanover Court) where he died in 1653.

The eighteenth century saw an increase in the number of lightermen, as trade in the Port of London grew; meanwhile the watermen's numbers diminished as yet more bridges were built. The waterman's wherry finally all but disappeared soon after the middle of the nineteenth century (although the title 'waterman' is still used for the crews of pleasure 'steamers') and today even the working lightermen are few in number, thanks to the diminishing barge traffic. But the Company of Watermen and Lightermen still flourishes, and administers the apprenticeship that is still demanded before a licence is given. A five years' indenture (seven years until quite recently) is required, and then the apprentice is examined rigorously before he is given his Lighterman's Licence. This qualifies him to handle a barge, and to be a tug captain when he has acquired the necessary experience. A Waterman's Licence now covers the 'steamers' (today diesel powered) which carry large numbers of passengers up and down the tideway between public piers, and this licence is only granted after a further and more stringent examination.

'WHO'S FOR THE FERRY?'

There is one waterman operating on the tideway whose work is very close to a waterman's job in John Taylor's day. His name is David Hastings, and from Easter until the autumn you may find him rowing passengers across the Thames at Twickenham Ferry.

The ferry between Twickenham and Ham House was granted in 1625 by Charles I to William Murray, first Lord Dysart, who lived at Ham. Between that date and the 1940s, the Dysarts continued as proprietors of the ferry; after the Second World War Ham House became the property of the nation, and the proprietorship of the ferry was acquired by the then ferryman, Harold Smoothey.

Dave Hastings, then a lad, was fascinated by the ferry, and used to help Mr Smoothey in the busy summer months. He was interested not least because the old man used a wherry, then ancient but just serviceable. Dave (who comes from a family long associated with the Thames) left school and became apprenticed as a lighterman to his grandfather, but just before the seven year apprenticeship was finished his grandfather died, and he found himself out of work (there were and are fewer and fewer jobs each year for apprentice lightermen). Harold Smoothey died too in 1963, so Dave Hastings came back to Twickenham Ferry and became the ferryman. He had a new wherry built (a rare thing indeed) by Bob Gibbs of Trowlock Island, and set to work.

He says he makes a living from it; the fare is 10p each way, and sometimes there are tips. Besides the visitors crossing from Twickenham to Ham House, a number of local people use the ferry to take them to and from work. He

Dave Hastings, the Twickenham ferryman, carrying passengers in the wherry *Charon*.

does not usually operate in the winter, but there are occasional commissions for special work, like the television series *Elizabeth R*, in which he ferried Glenda Jackson as Elizabeth I along the Thames. He also has a sideline in the form of a patent on a $1\frac{1}{2}$ hp steam engine, based upon drawings and an actual engine found in an attic. A friend constructs several of these each year for him, and they are sold principally for export.

Dave Hastings is by no means the only ferryman in these parts. There are a number of ferries between Hampton and Chiswick, mostly operating only in the summer months. But he regards himself as somewhat unique in that he is (to the best of his knowledge) the only Thames waterman still using a wherry, and the only one without a licence; he never completed his apprenticeship, and does not need to, thanks to the Royal Charter incorporating the ferry. In 1860 the Watermen's Company tried to oust one of his predecessors, the ferryman Cooper, because he, too, was unlicensed, but Cooper won the case. Dave Hastings points out with pride that his name is now on the royal documents (in the Victoria and Albert Museum), 'and I can do what I like and say what I like about the Company of Watermen and the Port of London Authority'. He preserves at home a manuscript of the old song about his ferry:

> O hoi ye ho, ho ye ho, who's for the ferry?
> The briar's in bud, the sun's going down,
> And I'll row ye so quick, and I'll row ye so steady,
> And 'tis but a penny to Twickenham Town.

The river Brent enters the Thames opposite Kew Gardens, and carries boats to and from the Grand Union Canal, which leads to Birmingham and the Midlands, and has a branch to Paddington and the Regent's Canal in London. Brentford Dock used to be situated in the Thames just upstream of the Brent Mouth, but it is now closed and the site is being built over. But a few hundred yards up the Brent itself is a thriving wharf operated by the British Waterways Board. Commodities handled include tea, lime juice and 'baby powder', and here, besides the barges which bring the cargoes up to Brentford from the docks down-river, you can also sometimes see canal narrow boats which carry the lime juice up the Grand Union to a factory at Boxmoor.

After Kew comes Chiswick Bridge and the finishing point of the annual Oxford and Cambridge Boat Race. In its early days the famous contest was not rowed here. The first race took place at Henley in 1829, on a two and a quarter mile course from Hambleden Lock to Henley Bridge, when Oxford were the winners. No match was arranged for the next six years because of a cholera epidemic and difficulty in agreeing where it was to be rowed, and the second race eventually took place in 1836, when it was rowed from Westminster to Putney, then the championship course for professionals. Cambridge were the winners, and this was the occasion when they first adopted light blue, Oxford having rowed in dark blue in 1829; one of the Cambridge supporters had bought a piece of light blue Eton ribbon from a shop and fixed it to the Cambridge bows for luck.

There were further races on the same course in the following years, but by 1845 there was so much traffic between Westminster and Putney that the race was rowed from Putney Bridge to Mortlake Church. The next year the finishing point was moved to the Ship Inn, Mortlake, and this has been the course (with a length of 4 miles 374 yards) which has been rowed ever since.

If you were very lucky you might, between the 1920s and the 1960s, have been invited to watch the Boat Race from A. P. Herbert's windows. Sir Alan Herbert, a great enthusiast for the Thames, lived from 1916 until his death in 1971 at 12 Hammersmith Terrace, one of the tall eighteenth century row of houses just below Chiswick Eyot. His interest in the river began when he acquired the house; soon he had learnt to sail, become a regular swimmer in the tideway, and acquired his first motor cruiser. His most famous boat was *Water Gipsy*, named after his successful novel about river and canal life *The Water Gipsies*. This little boat, built by Cole Brothers of Hammersmith in 1936, was a familiar sight on the tideway.

A.P.H. pursued an immensely successful career as an author, humorist and

Sir Alan Herbert near Thames Head.

playwright, best known for his contributions to *Punch* and his musical comedies. He was also an active Independent Member of Parliament, representing Oxford University for fifteen years from 1935, and often *Water Gipsy* carried him from Hammersmith to the House of Commons; sometimes after late sittings he would sleep on the boat, moored under the shadow of Westminster Bridge. He became firm friends with the lightermen and tug captains on the Thames, and is remembered by them with great affection. His celebrated Boat Race parties at Hammersmith Terrace could number up to 200 guests, who at various times included Clement Atlee, C. B. Cochran, H. G. Wells, Field Marshal Montgomery, and Charles Chaplin. ('Monty' once won sixpence from Chaplin when he backed Cambridge.)

Herbert was a Thames Conservator for many years, and was greatly concerned about the future of the river, in particular about the declining traffic on the tideway, the disappearance of the sailing barges, and the need for a Thames barrage, of which he was an early champion. He was closely associated with the Inland Waterways Association, and was a Freeman of the Company of Watermen and Lightermen. But it was the 1939–45 war that brought about his closest involvement with the Thames.

Strange things happened on the river during the war, not least in the summer of 1940, when the Dunkirk evacuation was hastily planned. Craft of all kinds were requisitioned from the tidal and non-tidal river, cruisers, yachts, sailing barges, and 'dumb' lighters to which motors were fitted. This strange conglomeration of vessels, some more seaworthy than others, made up a quarter of the Dunkirk fleet, the 'little ships' which evacuated over three hundred thousand men from France.

To A. P. Herbert's regret, *Water Gipsy* was not among them, for she had been 'commissioned' at the outbreak of war, and was part of the Royal Naval Thames (Auxiliary) Patrol, 'a kind of floating Home Guard' as he put it. By August 1940 she had been painted grey, given a machine gun, two revolvers, a box of hand grenades, and two cutlasses. A.P.H. was still Master (with the rank of Petty Officer), but there was now a naval crew on board, of whom the most notable member was Seaman Longstaff, who had a beard and a monocle. A.P.H. and Longstaff assisted at many of the crises on the river that eventful summer, but perhaps their finest hour was on 10 September when they went to help fight a fire at Lambeth. Longstaff wanted to try out the boat's new machine gun, so they moored just above Lambeth Bridge and he blazed away all night at enemy planes. This was not at all what the authorities had wanted, and there was an official uproar, with Herbert and Longstaff almost court-martialled. But A.P.H. remained unrepentant, and wrote many years later: 'I claim that the Battle of Lambeth Bridge was the most westerly action ever fought in the Thames under the White Ensign . . . There should be a plaque on the river-wall!'


### THE WANDLE, CHELSEA, AND SIR THOMAS MORE

By the Thames at Wandsworth there is a powerful smell of beer. Breweries have always needed a voluminous supply of water, and though the Thames long ago ceased to be an acceptable source of that supply, the brewery premises can still be seen sited on either side of the river in this area, occupying their original sites and in some cases still receiving their deliveries of grain by water. One of the breweries responsible for the Wandsworth smell, Young's Ram Brewery, is a few hundred yards away from the Thames itself, alongside the last upstream tributary left visible by the urban development of London, the River Wandle.

The Wandle has the distinction of having been mentioned in Izaak Walton's *Compleat Angler* as a good trout stream. Merton Abbey, where Thomas à Becket was educated, lay alongside it and enjoyed its supply of fish, and when William Morris opened his model factory at Merton in 1881, because of the suitability of the water for fabric dyeing, the trout could even be seen leaping outside the windows. In the previous century the poet Pope

148

The River Wandle beside Young's Ram Brewery at Wandsworth.

had called the river 'pure Vandalis', and Lord Nelson used to fish it at the bottom of Lady Hamilton's garden at Merton Place. She diverted part of the stream for ornamental purposes and liked to call this portion 'The Nile'.

But by the nineteenth century the Wandle was being polluted, encroached on, and urbanised. It found a champion just in time, in the person of John Ruskin, who wrote in eloquent damnation of its befoulers, and bought, restored and endowed a pool near its source in Carshalton. His action raised sufficient interest in the river for a society to be formed to carry on his work: the River Wandle Open Spaces Society. The number of parks and recreation grounds adjoining the Wandle is evidence of the society's success.

A mile below the mouth of the Wandle, an inlet on the north bank of the Thames gives barges access to a gasworks. This is all that remains of Chelsea or Counter's Creek, a stream that ran downwards from Kensal Green. In the 1820s the lowest mile and a quarter was made navigable as the Kensington Canal, but in the remaining years of the nineteenth century most of the canal was filled in and built over by a railway company. The last half mile remains as a waterway.

A few hundred yards below Chelsea Creek, under the shadow of Chelsea

Houseboats at Chelsea.

mill, is one of the river's principal 'houseboat villages', where several dozen craft of varying shapes and sizes are moored. The boats belong to the residents, who rent the moorings from a company with an office on one of the craft; the company also provides mains water and electricity. This arrangement is common on the lower part of the river. While there are no rates to be paid, rents here and at other moorings have risen considerably, and the houseboat dwellers say that soon they will be no better off financially than householders on land. A Residential Boat Owners' Association has recently been formed to protect the interests of houseboat dwellers in Britain.

The Chelsea houseboats are watched, from a few yards beyond Battersea Bridge, by the statue of Sir Thames More, who lived here for many years. In 1523, in his forty-sixth year, he bought land at Chelsea and built a celebrated house fronting the river by what is now Beaufort Street; it had a chapel, a library, and a gallery, as well as a spacious garden and orchard. (The house was pulled down in 1740.) Henry VIII used to like to walk by the river here when he visited More, who was his Lord Chancellor after the fall of Wolsey; and like Sir Alan Herbert four centuries later, More found the Thames a convenient route from his home to the Houses of Parliament.

More fell from favour after showing disapproval of Henry VIII's attempts to annul his first marriage. In 1534 he was summoned to Lambeth to swear an oath against the Pope; he refused, was imprisoned in the Tower, and executed the next year. William Roper, his son-in-law, describes in his Life of More the departure by boat to Lambeth which was, as it transpired, More's leave-taking of his home and family:

*Above:* Tug and lighters in Battersea Reach.
*Below:* Battersea Power Station at night.

And whereas he evermore used before, at his departure from his wife and children, whom he tenderlie loved, to have them bringe him to his boate, and there to kisse them, and bid them all farewell, then would he suffer none of them forth the gate to followe him, but pulled the Wickett after him, and shutt them all from him: and with a heavie heart, as by his countenance it appeared, with me and our fowre servants theare tooke boate towards *Lambethe*.

### FORGOTTEN TRIBUTARIES

Between Chelsea Bridge and the railway bridge just below it, you may be surprised to see a pair of lock gates. This is the entrance to what remains of the Grosvenor Canal, which used to reach up to a basin where Victoria Station now stands. Like the Kensington Canal, the Grosvenor was bought by a railway company and gradually built over. But the lowest section, a quarter of a mile long, remains as a truncated waterway and is used as a dock. Here, rubbish from the Westminster district is put in barges and towed down the estuary to be dumped in areas where land reclamation is going on. The Grosvenor dock has been used for this purpose since 1866; about eight barges a day leave it. More barges collect refuse from other points along the river.

Before the Grosvenor Canal was established, this inlet was a tidal creek. The Chelsea waterworks were established here in the 1720s, and introduced the first iron water-main in London. Their reservoir stood on the site which became the canal basin (the reservoir once froze over and got its owners into debt). Water was drawn partly from the Thames, by the aid of a tide-mill whose wheel turned when the tide flowed, and partly from the Westbourne, which was diverted just above its mouth in the grounds of Chelsea Hospital in order to feed the waterworks. London sightseers used to come and watch the company's Improved Newcomen pumping engine, but the Royal Family suffered its disadvantages when the smoke blew directly over Buckingham Palace.

That a river called the Westbourne should have partially supplied a large nineteenth-century reservoir in the heart of London would probably surprise most Londoners, who accept without much question the water-sounding suffixes, the bournes, brooks, mills, bridges and wells of so many of the capital's streets and districts. Even more surprising, perhaps, would be the fact that the Westbourne is still to be seen in the form of the Serpentine in Hyde Park, a lake formed when George II's wife, Queen Caroline, had the idea of damming the river a little north of the point where it was spanned by Knight's Bridge. And the underground railway traveller who happens to look up while he is waiting on the platform at Sloane Square Station can also

The River Westbourne carried in a culvert over Sloane Square Underground Station.

see the Westbourne, being carried over the line in a broad convex-bottomed culvert towards its confluence with the Thames in Chelsea.

The Westbourne, or Kilburn to give it its earlier name, is by no means the only Thames tributary that still flows in central London. The Tyburn, which gave its name to the place of execution, forms the lake in Regent's Park, and the windings of Marylebone Lane follow the course of the 'bone' or bourne itself, which can still sometimes be seen in basement excavations. Counter's Creek, which rose near Kensal Green Cemetery, can be seen off the King's Road, below which it is generally known as the Chelsea Creek. On the opposite bank of the Thames the Falcon appears as the short Battersea Creek after a subterranean journey from its springs in Balham and Tooting. The River Effra can still be seen for a few hundred yards near Dulwich Village, but the little bridges which used to lead over it to the houses along Brixton Road are now continuous pavement. Downstream on the south bank a brook flowed through Bermondsey, and its widened mouth made the St Saviour's Dock. Its name is the Neckinger, from the Neckinger wharf where Thames

Mouth of the Fleet, circa 1700, by Samuel Scott (*Guildhall Art Gallery*).

pirates were hung. The rope used to be known as the Devil's neckcloth or 'neckinger'.

There are still more streams which have disappeared under London. The Walbrook, which in its prime helped to fill the ditch surrounding London Wall (a part of this was notoriously full of dead dogs and so acquired the name Houndsditch) was last seen under the Bank of England. Among others which have vanished for all or part of their course are the Earl's Sluice in Rotherhithe, the Black Ditch between Stepney and Poplar, the Hackney Brook (a tributary of the Lea) and Parr's Ditch, Hammersmith Creek, and Stamford Brook in the west. And of all these tributaries, perhaps the one with the most curious and chequered history is the Fleet.

### TOSHERS AND TITTLEBATS

If you lean over the Embankment midway under the northern end of Black-friars Bridge, or better still look down to your left from the steps that lead up to the footway, you can see (if the tide is low enough) an arched opening in the Embankment wall. An iron ladder leads down to one side of the opening, which is some twenty feet broad. This is all that can now be seen in the centre of London of the river which was once the city's fortification, its water supply,

and its harbour, and was perhaps 600 feet wide at its mouth. You should go to Hampstead if you are interested in seeing the Fleet rise, an interest shared by Mr Samuel Pickwick, who delivered in 1827 to the Pickwick Club a paper of 'Speculation on the Source of the Hampstead Ponds, with some Observations on the Theory of Tittlebats'. It is the western branch, rising in the Vale of Health, that Dickens had in mind, but another branch appears as the ornamental lake in Kenwood, and forms the Highgate Ponds. The two streams join at Kentish Town, where an anchor was once found in the river bed, suggesting that the river may have been navigable here. St Pancras Way and Pancras Road next mark the course of the river as it makes its way down to Farringdon Street, carving a valley so deep that the Holborn Viaduct was built to span it.

The name 'Fleet' was in fact never applied to more than the tidal part nearest the Thames. (The word 'fleet' in this sense of tidal creek becomes common further down the Thames, at Benfleet and Charfleet on Canvey Island, at Northfleet, Fleet in Kent, and other places.) From Holborn Bridge upwards the river was non-tidal, and 'Hole burn' is the earliest recorded version of its name, the 'hole' referring to what was the then probably even more pronounced hollow in which it ran.

In mediæval times, the River Fleet was the natural defence for London on the western side; the Thames guarded the south, the marshes called Moorfields (from which the Walbrook sprang) guarded the north, and the Tower of London was built to defend the eastern corner. The notorious Fleet Prison appears first by name in 1197. Its moat was supplied partly by Fleet water, and its warder appears to have had the responsibility in the following century of controlling customs duty paid for goods brought up the Fleet, and for repairing the bridge that carried what became known as Fleet Street over the river. In the Middle Ages the Fleet carried stones for the building of Old St Paul's, coal from Newcastle-on-Tyne to the wharf at the end of Seacoal Lane (first so named in 1228), contraband cargoes of Welsh cheese, wine to the Fleet Prison, and patients to St Bartholomew's Hospital.

But like the Trill Mill Stream in Oxford, the Fleet was also used for sewage and refuse disposal, and the stench from it had by 1290 become unbearable. There were attempts to clean it up, but disease still flourished, and when the Great Plague struck the now sprawling city in 1665, the squalid households surrounding this open sewer were among the worst afflicted.

When Sir Christopher Wren was appointed to reconstruct London after the Great Fire the following year, the memory of both its disease and its advantages led him to give the Fleet a grand role in his plan. Its last 2,100 feet were to become an elegant and valuable canal. So the river was dredged, widened to 50 feet, and given broad 30 foot wharves on either side. The bridges Wren designed over it were high and Italianate, but the spaces under their ramps were given practical use as storage vaults. But for all the sense in it, Wren's idea did not prosper. The human instinct of dumping rubbish in the nearest open water prevailed, and the wharfage charges never yielded enough to ensure regular dredging. The public preferred to park their goods and vehicles on the spacious wharves, and even the space taken by the water itself was soon wanted for other uses. Less than eighty years after it was proposed, the Fleet Canal was covered as far as Fleet Street and a market built over it. After another thirty years the remaining part of the river had disappeared from view. In 1829 the market was pulled down to make way for a broad new street called Farringdon Street.

Covering the Fleet by no means adequately protected the city from the waste the river still carried. When it flooded, the sewage reappeared above ground, and it nurtured the water-borne infection of cholera, causing epidemics in such nearby places as Clerkenwell Prison. Yet for all its filth there was a strange living to be won from the Fleet in Victorian times. Men known as 'toshers' used to wade into its mouth at low tide and go up, sometimes all the way to Camden Town, gathering the coins and other valuables that had dropped down from the streets above.

Other buried rivers had the same function as the Fleet and emptied their effluent directly into the Thames in London, it being trusted that the tide would in time bear it away. There were even latrines on the banks of the

'The Fleet today, near its mouth under Blackfriars Bridge (*G.L.C.*)'

Thames discharging immediately into the main river. (Fishermen used to tie their boats to them. The mooring ropes often tripped up passers-by and pulled down the latrines.)

The weakness of this as the sewage system for a great city was well known. But the legislators did nothing about it until the celebrated year when the matter forced itself quite literally under their noses. In 1858, the Year of the Great Stink, the Houses of Parliament had to have window-curtains soaked in chloride of lime in order that the Members could breathe and work there. Sewage reform was quickly initiated.

Under the new system, which remains essentially unchanged, there are purpose built sewers discharging far down the estuary. The Fleet and the other underground rivers have become storm relief sewers, carrying almost entirely surface water. In dry weather they are not spectacular, but after a heavy rain they can fill very quickly and rush with all their old force. But no river can be completely culverted. While its main stream may run in a continuous pipe, small tributaries which once joined it freely are now thwarted. In all probability they still use the old and natural watercourse, and gather to form a 'shadow river' of their own.

There was once a study made of places in London reputed to be haunted. A remarkable number of these turned out to be in the vicinity of one of the buried streams, and so it was suggested that what often sounded like a ghostly footstep or the swishing of a silken skirt was in fact the noise of a 'lost' river down below.

London Bridge in 1760: a hazard to navigation.

LONDON BRIDGE

Under the shadow of Big Ben you can step on to a hydrofoil and go on a high speed journey down the river to Greenwich. London Hoverservice Ltd have been operating a regular schedule of journeys between Westminster, Charing Cross, Tower and Greenwich Piers since 1973. The service (subsidised by the government and the Greater London Council) is principally intended for commuters (although it can also be used by visitors), many of whom make regular use of it. It is a fast service but it is liable to be delayed or cancelled in bad weather. The journey is on the bumpy side, and the windows are heavily tinted ('to keep out the glare' said a stewardess), so that if you want a good view of the tideway you would do better to travel on one of the many pleasure 'steamers' that ply between the various public piers.

As you pass Hungerford, Waterloo, Southwark and Blackfriars Bridges it is surprising to remember that until the middle of the eighteenth century, London Bridge was the only bridge in the capital. The first London Bridge may have existed in the time of the Roman occupation; certainly there was a crossing here in the tenth century A.D. It featured in a fight between Æthelred and the Danes in 1014, was burnt down and rebuilt in the middle of the twelfth century, and rebuilt again in the early thirteenth. The bridge of that date, which was made of stone, possessed nineteen pointed arches, and had buildings on it. In 1358 there were 138 shops on the bridge, and a chapel dedicated to St Thomas à Becket. In 1240 a whale 'of prodigious size' swam through one of the arches, and was pursued and finally killed at Mortlake. In the next century the custom began of exposing the heads of executed men on the bridge (Sir Thomas More's head suffered this fate in 1535). In 1536 an

Hydrofoil on the tideway.

apprentice named Osborne rescued an infant, Anne Hewet, who had fallen from a window on the bridge into the river. He later married her and afterwards became Lord Mayor of London.

The wooden platforms (known as 'starlings') that protected the piers caused a dangerous current between the arches, and gave rise to the saying 'London Bridge was made for wise men to go over and fools to go under'. Many travellers disembarked at the bridge and dragged their boats round; Wolsey would not dare to go under it, but Henry VIII sometimes did. The sound of the rushing water was considerable, and it was increased when in 1582 a Dutchman installed water mills on the bridge. But when the houses were removed by Act of Parliament in the 1750s, a gentleman who had once lived on the bridge (a haberdasher aged 71 called Baldwin), found himself unable to sleep in his new home because he missed the noise of the waters.

The bridge was replaced by an entirely new structure in 1831, and this bridge in its turn gave way recently to a four million pound bridge paid for by the City Corporation of London, and opened by the Queen in 1973. The previous bridge was sold and has been re-erected stone by stone in Los Angeles.

### DOGGETT'S COAT AND BADGE RACE

Just upstream of London Bridge, overlooking the river from the north bank, is a nineteenth-century building in the grand classical manner. This is Fish-

Westminster.

mongers' Hall, home of the Worshipful Company of Fishmongers, one of the ancient Livery Companies of the City of London, and one of the oldest Guilds (it was granted its first charter in 1272). Here, on ceremonial occasions, you may see a splendidly dressed figure in a maroon coat and breeches with a huge gold badge on his arm, and a cocked hat on his head: Charles Frank Taylor, Bargemaster to the Fishmongers' Company and one of the most knowledgeable men about the tideway. He is also Deputy Bargemaster to Her Majesty the Queen and the organiser of the celebrated Doggett's Coat and Badge Race.

Charles Taylor was born in Battersea before the First World War, and began work in 1921 at the age of fourteen with Humphery & Grey, a lighterage company, which was then based at Hay's Wharf on the South Bank between London and Tower Bridges; his father and brothers also worked for the firm. A lighterage firm handles barges, nowadays chiefly towing them with tugs. But in those days, and until quite recent times, lightermen would often be called on to row or 'drive' a barge with huge oars or 'sweeps'. The lighterman would row standing up at one end of the barge, with an apprentice to help him if the load was more than fifty tons. The barge could be 'driven' for as long as the tide would help to carry it: for five hours on a flood tide, for seven on an ebb. Sometimes the barges would have to be 'driven' at night from one dock or buoy to another, with perhaps no more than a candle in a jam jar for a navigation light. Often the lightermen would end their working day miles away from the home wharf, and have to make their own way back.

Charles Taylor served his seven year apprenticeship with the Company of

Charles Taylor in Bargemaster's livery at Fishmongers' Hall.

Watermen and Lightermen, and eventually was examined for his Lighterman's licence, answering questions about the river, the tides, and the handling of barges. And as his apprenticeship came to an end, he decided to make an attempt to win the Doggett's Coat and Badge Race.

Thomas Doggett, who died in 1721, was an Irish comedian, and like all players he depended on the services of the London watermen who ferried him to and fro between engagements, and also carried the audience who came to see him. He was a staunch Hanoverian, and wished to mark the anniversary of the accession of George I, so in 1715 he offered 'an orange coloured livery . . . to be rowed for by six watermen that are out of their time within a year past' (that is, who had completed their apprenticeship during the preceding twelve months). 'They are,' the announcement concluded, 'to row from London Bridge to Chelsea. It will be continued, annually, on the same day forever.'

The race has indeed been rowed annually ever since, in July (the actual date depends on tide conditions), and it is believed to be the oldest annual sporting event surviving in the world. Certainly it is the world's longest rowing race, with a course one furlong short of five miles.

In its heyday there might be as many as three hundred entrants, of whom only six were allowed to row, their names being drawn by lot. In the 1920s there was still tremendous competition to gain the coveted Coat and Badge— and the prize money, for it was then still a 'professional' race, and the year before Charles Taylor's apprenticeship ended he went into hard training. Competitors had to row in their own boats, and an impecunious apprentice

Waterman in Doggett's livery.

would be hard put to buy one; he managed to acquire a second-hand 'best boat', as the racing boats were called, for twelve pounds. In the five weeks before the 1929 race he would walk twenty miles or row forty miles each day, and stayed with friends in Putney, 'because the air is better up there'. The expense of it all was considerable, and he knew he would have to win to be able to pay his bills.

He won, even though a member of the celebrated Phelps family was rowing against him, and almost all the Phelps's have won the race. The prize was twenty pounds in cash, the vermilion livery with its silver buttons, the cap, the breeches, and the silver badge on which is embossed the famous White Horse of Hanover and the words 'The gift of Mr Thomas Doggett, the late famous Comedian. Winner 1929 Charles Frank Taylor'.

Back at work, Charles Taylor soon became a tug captain. In all, he com-

Four winners of Doggett's Coat and Badge: left to right, Harry Phelps, Bert Barry, Charles Taylor and Kenneth Everest (*Keystone Press Agency*).

pleted forty-eight years' service with Humphery & Grey, ending up as labour master with thirteen foremen and 200 lightermen answerable to him. And when his retirement came, he was able to continue his association with the tideway.

He had become a Royal Waterman in 1951, after making an application to St James's Palace accompanied by testimonials. He has always been involved with the Company of Watermen and Lightermen, and in 1968 he became their Bargemaster. Then in 1973, after the death of the previous holder of that office, Harry Phelps, he became Bargemaster to the Worshipful Company of Fishmongers.

In past centuries the City Companies, like Royalty, made great use of barges or shallops, and many City occasions involved their use; there was a water procession as part of Lord Mayor's Day from 1422 until 1856, and in the eighteenth century waterborne music became fashionable. The *Daily Courant* reported an occasion in July 1717 when there could be seen on the Thames 'a City Company's barge . . . wherein were fifty instruments of all sorts, who played all the way from Lambethe the finest symphonies, composed express for this occasion by Mr Hendel.' Handel's Water Music was probably simply a collection of these occasional pieces composed for water picnics and royal parties.

In the 1850s water processions ceased and the company barges were laid up, chiefly because by then the Thames at London was filthy and stinking with sewage. But the office of Bargemaster continued with the Watermen's and Fishmongers' Companies, with ceremonial duties attached to the post, although the ceremony is usually on dry land. Charles Taylor in his handsome livery as Fishmongers' Bargemaster officiates at banquets and Royal visits, and obviously gets a good deal of enjoyment out of it all.

Since he began his working life the tideway has changed almost beyond recognition; lightermen no longer 'drive' barges, many of the old firms have closed, and even the huge Hay's Wharf is shut and awaiting redevelopment. Tilbury has taken a large proportion of traffic from the Pool of London, and Charles Taylor's second son, who is a tug captain for Humphery & Grey, does much of his work at Tilbury Grain Terminal. The number of competitors for Doggett's Coat and Badge has greatly decreased, and some years there are no more than three or four men rowing. The Fishmongers' Company, which has administered the race for many years, provides the boats, and the race now has 'amateur' status, with silver cups substituted for the prize money. But despite the changes in its character, the race still carries great prestige, and many Doggett's winners go on to achieve success at international events. Charles Taylor, as Fishmongers' Bargemaster, makes all the arrangements for the race, and he is quite sure that 'it will be continued, annually, upon the same day forever'.

TRAFFIC FROM THE SEA

In its heyday as a gaol, the Tower of London received many of its prisoners by water. One such was the Princess Elizabeth who in 1554, on a rainy Palm Sunday, was brought by barge to Traitor's Stairs; she had been accused of treachery against her sister Mary. On 19 May she was taken from the Tower to Richmond, again by water; thinking her freed (which she was not) the Thames steelyard merchants fired salvoes of artillery in her honour. She, the future queen, was one of the Tower's most eminent prisoners; many others arrived by water never to leave again.

And the Tower still occasionally features in history. In February 1965 after Sir Winston Churchill's funeral at St Paul's Cathedral, his body was brought to Tower Stairs, whence a launch carried it up the river to Waterloo Pier; from Waterloo Station it was taken to Bladon churchyard. The dockyard cranes were dipped in salute.

Tower Bridge (built in 1894) is the last bridge before the sea; nowadays it only opens its bascules occasionally as fewer and fewer large ships venture above the Millwall Docks. The Pool of London sees little commercial traffic now. The two principal dock areas here, St Katharine by the Tower and

164

Sailing barge in St Katharine's Dock; the Tower Hotel beyond.

AN
Exact and lively View
or
REPRESENTATION
Of Booths and all the varieties of showes
Humours upon the ICE on the River
THAMES by LONDON
During that memorable Frost in the 2
of the Reigne of our Sovereigne
Lord King GEORGE.
Anno Dⁿⁱ MDCCXVI.

With an Alphabetical Explanation of the
most remarkeable Figures

The Temple Staires with People goeing donne upon the Ice to Temple Street A.
press printer just by new Thames Street C. The Turners Booth in New Thames Street with
Stands D. The Roast Beefe Booth E. The Halfe way house F. The Silver Smith Boe
Booth I. The Lottery Booth K. The Cutlers Booth L. The Temple Walks with Croud:
Ware Booth N. The Coffee house O. The Chopp house Booth P. The wrestling ring Q.
it R. The boys Sliding S. The Nine Pinn Playing T. The Scaters V. The Leather Be
London Bridge Z.

London Sold by Iohn Lenthall Stationer at the

thers Booth in Temple Street B. The Rowling
l & Hand insured as long as the foundation
e Musick Booth H. The Comon printing press
le looking over the wall M. The Tunbridge
Sheep roasted and Crouds of People round
h W. The Drum Booth X. The Toy Shopps Y.

st S.t Dunstans Church in Fleet street London. Price Six pence

Frost Fair on the Thames above London
Bridge, 1716. The river often froze while
the old bridge restricted its flow (*Bodleian
Library*).

Sailing barge loaded with hay, opposite the Custom House, before 1914.

London Docks (both on the north bank below Tower Bridge) were closed in 1968 and 1969 respectively. They used to specialize in wool and wine. The London Docks have been partially filled in, and their fine early nineteenth-century warehouses stand idle. The exact future of this part of dockland is still under discussion, and there is a great deal of local pressure for any redevelopment to include council housing. Expensive flats are meanwhile being created by private developers in old wharf buildings in Wapping.

The St Katharine's Dock redevelopment is nearing completion. A World Trade Centre has been established here and will be partly housed in Thomas Telford's 1828 warehouses; the Port of London Authority has moved its headquarters to the dock, and overlooking them is a new hotel, almost big enough to dwarf the Tower. St Katharine's Dock (after much controversy) will also include 700 dwellings, 300 of them to be let by the Greater London Council. The dock itself is being used for yacht moorings, and also provides a home for an exhibition of historic craft. Already moored here is the former Nore lightship, now open to the public, and you may also be lucky enough to see in the dock one or two specimens of an almost extinct race, the Thames sailing barge.

The building of the docks in London in the early nineteenth century created a need for a small vessel that could handle coastal traffic. So the estuary sailing barge came into being, a true sailing vessel as distinct from the more primitive up-river barges which sometimes used sails but were often towed. The sailing barges carried many cargoes, but specialised in hay, other agricultural products, and building materials. They were generally eighty feet long with a beam of twenty feet, had flat bottoms and were straight-sided with a round bow and a transom stern, and they could carry 120 tons of cargo. The seventy to eighty foot mast supported 3,000 square feet of sail, so the barges were a striking sight when under way. Lee boards could be let down to aid stability. The sailing barges declined with the development of motorised road transport, and only 140 were still under sail after the Second World War. Many have now been broken up, some are preserved as house-boats, and a few are still kept in working trim, and can be seen in sailing barge matches.

St Katharine's Dock also provides a home for the Dutch motor barge *Res Nova*, which at present serves as a floating shop. Here the proprietor, Hilary Peters, will sell you (among other things) goat's cheese, yoghurt, fruit juice, duck eggs, and desk-top gardens.

The Surrey Docks, on the south bank adjoining Rotherhithe, were closed in 1970, and are desolate at present. The small Regent's Canal Dock at Limehouse opposite, which gives access to the country's inland waterways network and was once busy with canal narrow boats trading to and from the Midlands, is still open but now sees very little traffic. Real dockland activity now only starts at Millwall on the Isle of Dogs.

The 'Isle' (really a spit of land surrounded by a great meander of the river) was open country and marsh until 1799, when Parliament authorised the building of a new dock here to ease overcrowding in the Port of London. The West India Docks were opened in 1802, the Millwall in 1864, and the South Dock in 1870. Modernisation here in recent years has provided up-to-date transit sheds, electric cranes and fork-lift trucks. The main imports handled here are fresh and dried fruit, vegetables, grain, wood, sugar, paper pulp and boards, hides and skins, canned goods, rubber, hemp and wine. The Port of London Authority's bulk wine terminal in the West India Docks can store nearly a million gallons.

The Thames turns sharply north at the foot of the Isle of Dogs, and soon reaches the Royal Docks which, with a water area of 230 acres, are among the biggest in the world. The Royal Victoria (1855), the Royal Albert (1880), and the King George V (1921) can receive some of the largest general cargo ships, and handle trade from all parts of the world, including Russia and the Far East. Imports include meat and dairy products; exports include motor vehicles, machinery and steel, spirits and manufactured goods. The whole group of docks is over two and a half miles long. But like the India and Millwall Docks, their long term future is by no means certain.

Industrial disputes in recent years have not contributed to the prosperity of these docks; a more positive factor in their decline (and in the decline of the docks that have already been closed) is the growth of container traffic.

The basic principle of containers is very simple: the bulking together in one box of items of cargo that would otherwise have to be handled individu-ally. The same containers can be used for road, rail or water transport, and

Aerial view of the Royal Docks, showing the Royal Albert Dock and the smaller King George V Dock in the 1960s (*P.L.A.*).

Handling containers at Tilbury Dock (*P.L.A.*).

their size is only limited by the smallest vehicle in the transport chain, normally the lorry or rail wagon.

Container cargoes can be handled much faster than conventional 'loose' cargoes; ships can even be loaded and unloaded simultaneously. But special cranes and extra large stacking areas are needed, and the Port of London Authority has provided them at Tilbury, on the north bank of the Thames in Essex, about twenty-five miles downstream of London Bridge. Here containers up to forty feet long are loaded on to road or rail trailers by 'straddle carriers' very different in appearance from the familiar dock cranes. In consequence ships can turn round here in thirty-six hours, compared with ten to fourteen days if cargo has to be unloaded item by item. It is scarcely surprising that Tilbury is growing while the conventional docks up-river decline.

Another feature of the P.L.A.'s Tilbury development is a huge new grain terminal on the riverside itself. Up to 2,000 tons per hour can be unloaded by suction from ships and 'blown' into waiting barges or coasters, or passed into the silo building which has a storage capacity of 100,000 tons.

Tilbury was selected for development because it is outside the congested London road network; the Dartford Tunnel under the river gives access to the South and West of England, while other roads provide easy routes to northbound motorways.

But Tilbury is not the end of the story, nor the end of the Thames. A giant new deepwater seaport terminal has been planned by the P.L.A. for Maplin Sands, and it seems certain that the trend to site new docks down-river and

Unloading from ship to barge with a floating crane (*P.L.A.*).

A river police patrol boat below Tower Bridge circa 1900 (*Metropolitan Police*).

away from London will continue.

Years ago the Thames estuary was a passenger highway as well as a thoroughfare for cargo. Shipping companies operated regular schedules to all parts of the world, while on a more modest level, day trips to the South Coast were popular as outings for Londoners. Today there are passenger services from Tilbury to Sweden, Finland, Russia and the Canary Isles. But only one company still has passenger ships sailing from London itself: every Thursday a ship of the Fred Olsen Line leaves the Milwall Docks, bound for Madiera, Lanzarote, Tenerife and Las Palmas. The dock provides full customs and immigration facilities. Perhaps with the decline of cargo traffic in the Pool of London, more companies may follow this example and use the docks as a passenger terminal handy for the metropolis.

### POLICING THE RIVER

An old-fashioned blue lamp marks the entrance to the police station in Wapping High Street, but the building's more important approach is by water, for this is the headquarters of the Thames Division of the Metropolitan Police.

The first river police force in London was a semi-official body formed by the West India Company of Merchantmen to protect their cargoes from

A police duty boat leaves Thames Division headquarters at Wapping (*Metropolitan Police*).

pilfering. It began operations on the present Wapping site in 1798, and although the Merchantmen staffed the Water Police and Watchmen, there was also an official resident Magistrate, John Harriott. The new force had its work cut out, for nearly one third of all port workers at the time were known to be thieves or receivers of stolen property, and some ships entering the Port had as much as half their cargo made away with.

In 1839 the river force was incorporated into the Metropolitan Police as Thames Division. Nearly a century and a half later it is doing the same job, though with more up to date equipment: the rowing and sailing boats originally used for patrols were replaced in 1910 by motor craft, and today there are 30 'duty boats' with 100 bhp engines. Each of these is manned by three men, one as coxswain, one as radio-telephone operator in contact with New Scotland Yard, and one as 'deck hand' facing towards the stern and keeping a lookout behind.

The patrols cover fifty-four miles of river from Staines Bridge to Dartford Creek, and there are seven Thames police stations, one of which, at Waterloo Pier, is the famous floating police station. The Wapping headquarters include a well-equipped workshop where the thirty foot glass-fibre duty boats are lifted up hydraulically from the river and serviced. Here too is the museum housing relics of Thames Division's early days, lovingly collected by P.C. John Joslin, the Division's unofficial historian, and open to visitors by written arrangement. Here you can see the early uniform, one feature of which is still preserved in the 'lower deck reefer' double-breasted jacket worn since 1841 by the river police.

As the commercial traffic on the tideway has declined, so has the variety and number of incidents involving the river police, and often Thames Division's black and cream patrol launch is the only boat moving between Tower Bridge and Wapping. But there are still plenty of calls on the division's services, not least to act as rescuers for the many suicide attempts along the river. Each boat carries first aid equipment which includes a resuscitator for artificial respiration.

The river police also have an unofficial watching brief on potential pollution hazards. This, though, is chiefly the responsibility of the Port of London Authority.

In the late 1950s the tideway was evil-smelling, virtually without oxygen, and full of all kinds of chemical pollutants. Fish were unable to survive, and the only birds to be found were a few mute swans, mallard, gulls and pigeons. At that time the P.L.A. and the Greater London Council initiated anti-pollution measures: the construction of a new sewage works, the setting-up of oxygenation plants, and the establishment of a monitoring organisation. By 1963 oxygen was found to be present in the water throughout the whole year for the first time; by 1972 a total of sixty-six different species of fish had been found in the previously fishless zones of the inner Thames. The situation is constantly improving.

PUTTING UP THE BARRIER

Opposite the most southerly point of the Isles of Dogs, just upstream of Greenwich, lies the mouth of Deptford Creek, which is the name given to the tidal part of the river Ravensbourne. In the Creek Henry VIII founded his Royal Dockyard in 1513, and here Drake entertained Elizabeth I on board the *Golden Hinde* after his voyage around the world. The Queen commanded that the ship should thereafter be kept in honourable retirement in the Creek. Shipping still has legal precedence when entering Deptford Creek, and can halt the Southern Electric trains which cross the creek by moveable bridge on their way to and from neighbouring Greenwich.

Sir Alan Herbert thought Greenwich 'about the best advertisement for monarchy that exists'. Here was a mediæval palace and the first of the Royal parks. Henry VIII hawked and hunted there and watched his navy being built in the Dockyards at Deptford next door, and at nearby Woolwich. His daughters Mary and Elizabeth were born at Greenwich. It was a time when errands were best run by water; an account survives for the hire of a boat from Greenwich to London for the sake of the future Queen Elizabeth, then aged three 'to take measure of caps for my lady Princess and again to fetch the Princess's purple satin cap and to mend it'. In May 1536 Elizabeth's mother, Anne Boleyn, was taken from Greenwich Palace to the Tower to await her execution, in a barge that had once belonged to the woman she had supplanted, Katharine of Aragon.

Greenwich was abandoned as a royal palace at the end of the seventeenth century, but one earlier royal house there survived the extravagantly Baroque rebuilding programme of that time. It is the one built by Inigo Jones for Queen Anne of Denmark and known as the Queen's House. Preserved, too, is its view of the river. Dividing the buildings which now house the Royal Naval College is a gap 115 feet wide, through which the Queen's House looks at the Thames, and equally water travellers see the house to its best advantage. A little downstream of Greenwich, almost opposite Blackwall Point at the tip of the river's next meandering loop, the Thames is joined by its most navigable tributary: the Lea (in fact the navigation entrance is via a dock at Old Ford). Then, a little further down, at the beginning of Woolwich Reach, two signs on either bank face the river and each other, advertising work taking place there on the Greater London Council's flood protection barrier.

London and the south-east of England are sinking, at a rate clearly perceptible from records kept over the last 180 or so years. In 1791 a tide reaching almost fourteen feet above ordnance sea level at London bridge was exceptionally high. In 1881 a high tide level well over two feet higher was recorded at the same place. In 1928 fourteen people were drowned when the high tide reached seventeen feet above sea level. Flood defences were built well above this in the next few years, but the sea surged over them in 1953, drowning 309 people (and reaching nearly eighteen feet above sea level). The tipping of Britain like some vast see-saw (by which, incidentally, the north-east of Scotland really does get the advantage) is not the only factor. As with the non-tidal river, the more land is drained, and barricaded against the rising water, the more sudden and serious the flooding of the only places where the river may still go. The draining and embanking of upstream water-meadows has something of the same effect as the reclamation of the esturial salt-marshes. In 1953 Central London was only saved from crippling floods because the water spread out over the low-lying lands at the mouth of the estuary. Fifty-three of the drowned were on Canvey Island. Since that disaster the Kent and Essex coasts have been developed and more securely embanked, and every year the statistical likelihood has increased of an exceptionally high tide, whipped up by air pressure at sea and northerly gales, arriving at London with its force unspent.

The prospect has appalled all those who have thought about it. The underground railway throughout Central London would be flooded; power supplies, telephones, sewerage and water systems would all be unuseable.

Some forty-five square miles of London lie below the level that the tide reached in 1953: if London were to take the force of a flood reaching above that level, a strip of varying width along the whole length of the tidal Thames, including half of Hammersmith, Kensington and Chelsea, most of Southwark, and almost the whole of dockland, would be below water.

Considering the length of time the possibility of such floods has been recognised, it is extraordinary how long it has taken to put any major precautions into effect. Part of the trouble was that the committee reporting on the 1953 floods recommended some form of permanent structure right across the river, either a dam with locks, or a moveable barrier, and the argument over exactly which it should be then raged for years. Finally, by 1971, the Greater London Council had decided on a barrier, one which would present no obstacle to shipping in normal conditions, but which would rise to stem a surging tide at short notice. For the time being, the G.L.C. signboards and the works beneath them in the Woolwich Reach are all that can be seen of what will eventually (in normal conditions) look like an unfinished bridge. There will be a series of piers up to 200 feet apart with nothing normally appearing to connect them. Meteorological stations along the coast of England already keep watch for the signs of surging seas heading for the bottleneck of the Channel. When the barrier is finished their warnings will be able to lead to the barrier gates turning on an axis, rising from their position flat on the Thames bed, and standing upright, all in an estimated fifteen minutes. Downstream of the barrier, the bank will have to be raised in outer London and all along the Kent and Essex shore.

The cost of the scheme (excluding the Kent and Essex works) was estimated in 1970 at £75,000,000, to be paid partly by the G.L.C. and partly by a government grant. The cost of a London flood, if no barrier were to prevent it, was harder to calculate. The G.L.C. hazarded a guess of £1,000 million in 1971, not counting the loss of life. But the barrier looks like being some years more in the building. In the meanwhile the business of adding a few inches to various places on the Embankment goes on continuously. Public places in dockland and other vulnerable areas have posters setting out the flood procedure: alert symbols, then sirens and news on the radio direct from the London Flood room. But if all this is a match for any floods that happen between now and the day the barrier is finished, it will be more a matter of good luck than anything else.

THE BARGE-ROADS

At intervals all along the Thames below Brentford you can notice groups of barges. For the most part they seem to have an air of being carefully aban-

Lighterman at work at a barge-road.

doned, sheeted down and securely fastened, part of the immoveable furniture of the Thames. If you return some days later, it may seem that the same barges are still there, but if you look more closely, though the colours and company name may be the same, the names of many of the individual barges will have changed, and perhaps some will be lying higher or lower in the water than they were before. This slow changing place of barges, laden and unladen, and the occasional sight of a tug pulling them from one place to another, is all the evidence generally visible to the public of the business of lighterage.

The task of the lighterman, fetching and carrying where larger ships cannot go, is still performed for the most part in the way it has been ever since powered tugs finally predominated over rowing, or 'driving', and the sailing barge. On the river in London all but a handful of the tugs are small, squat, well-fendered vessels, with an apparently disproportionate distance between the spartan cabin and the low-lying stern; the reason for this being the need for a towing point as near amidships as possible. For every tug in its fleet, a lighterage firm will have scores of unpowered barges or lighters, each at least seventy-five feet long and twenty feet broad, with simple fixed rudders so that they tow easily and can be set loose to glide smoothly to a predetermined point under their own momentum. Thames barges have completely flat bottoms, so that they may sit easily on the foreshore, and still be loaded and unloaded when the tide is out; and a sloping 'prow' at each end called the 'swim', by which the wash from the tug's propeller escapes with the least resistance from the following barge. Although all barges are similar in outward appearance, some are adapted or specially designed for particular types of load. Hay's Wharf, for instance, used to specialise in cold storage, and insulated barges were built for this branch of the trade. When business fell off, some of the insulated barges, unsuitable for anything else, were made into pontoons, fixed at the various mooring points.

When a barge is not being loaded or unloaded, or towed from one place to another, it is kept at a buoy or mooring point. There are very many of these, distributed all along the commercial reaches of the tideway. A few are open to all comers, and crowded, but most are rented by individual companies from the Port of London Authority. These mooring points are known as 'roads', and to the tugman their names are familiar. These are the names he will find on the work sheet that tells him where he must collect the barges for his day's towage duties.

The working hours of a lighterman used to depend entirely on the time of the tides, whose ebb and flow were used for all barge navigation before the days of tugs, and are still invaluable as a free source of energy and saver of expensive fuel. In recent years the working hours of lightermen have altered considerably, and now the great majority of the men are on shift-work. But, since the 1950s, all other changes have been overshadowed by the decline in cargoes to the Port of London, and consequently of lighterage itself.

Every lighterman has his own analysis of the reasons for the decline; the generally acknowledged elements are the shift to lorry transport and particularly to containers, the failure of the docks to modernise soon enough, reluctance to let hard-pressed companies make men redundant, and strikes. Among men who have worked for more than twenty years on the river there is a prevailing nostalgia for the days when, though the work was much harder, the Thames was really busy and thriving, and the P.L.A. magazine cover boasted that a ship sailed from London to every port in the world. The lightermen's own union disappeared with that trade: the numbers of members of the Lightermen, Bargemen, & Tugmen's Union, as it was called, dwindled to about two thousand, before it was amalgamated into the Transport & General Workers' Union. But for those who are left in the lighterage trade, the pay is good, and compares well with (say) a car-worker's. A man working a fifteen hour shift will come to work only on five days in a fortnight, and overnight work is comparatively rare. Nevertheless the fear of unemployment remains. Every so often a lighterage firm goes out of business, and those firms that remain are not often able to absorb the redundant men.

One of the companies that has survived is Humphery & Grey (Lighterage) Ltd., Charles Taylor's old firm. This firm has over 130 barges, uses 5 tugs, and employs about 100 men, carrying for the most part bulk grain. Recently the company has also become involved in the distribution of LASH lighters throughout the tideway. These LASHcraft (the letters stand for Lighter

179

Aboard Ship) are giant oblong floating containers, sixty feet long and thirty feet wide, which are lifted off a 'mother ship' further down the estuary, and then brought under tug-power to London, where their cargoes, up to 400 tons in each craft, are discharged. Although the LASHcraft are more like steel boxes than boats, and have no grace compared with the traditional Thames lighter, they are broader and carry a greater tonnage. They were designed for pushing rather than pulling, and when handled in this way by a specially designed 'pushing tug' they move easily through the water, since the wash from the tug is behind the convoy, and does not hinder the tow. Thames tugs are limited by the Port of London Authority to a maximum of six barges, be they pushed or pulled.

The use of the steel box type of craft is well suited to the carriage of containers, and with the increasing use of containers for the transport of cargo by sea, it seems inevitable that the LASHcraft and similar vessels will be used more and more. Another development has been the construction of the BACAT (Barge Aboard Catamaran) ship, which carries between Britain and the Continent ten 140-ton compartment boats and three LASH lighters. LASHcraft are also being carried between the United States and Europe.

GREY LASH

Humphery & Grey's own LASHcraft pushing tug, *Grey Lash*, had been in service for two months when we joined her crew for part of a day's work early in 1975. Skipper for that day was David Humphries, deputising for the usual captain. Acting as his mate was Bill Rhoden, a man very much of the old school of lightermen, who has worked for many firms during a long career on the tideway.

*Grey Lash* carries an engineer; that day it was Peter Hovell. He is responsible for looking after the two 'caterpillar' 360 bhp engines. The boat has no rudders: steering is entirely by means of the two propellors, and the tug can move sideways as easily as forward or astern.

Under the most recent labour agreement a tug carries a number of 'domicile men' who are attached to it for the whole of a shift, and make up the rest of the crew; more towing hands are collected en route, so that at any time there should be roughly one man to each barge being towed.

The towing instructions received when the shift started at seven that morning gave the times of the day's high tides, and then the list of barges, destinations and hands: a domiciled hand (Leonard Powell) to be picked up from Fountain Roads, *Grey Bear* to be taken from Chalkstone Roads to Lower Roads at Charles Hays', and so on to fill the day. As it happened

Tug *Grey Lash* at Cherry Garden Pier.

all the work that day involved conventional towing, as there were no 'Lashcraft' to be handled, but *Grey Lash* is also well equipped to tow.

One of the instructions was to be ready for various maintenance engineers to come on board and check the tug's still very new fittings and equipment. Since the days when the watermen's wherries plied from all the public stairs along the Thames, the tideway has become sadly enclosed, with most of its traditional points of access fenced and padlocked. An exception is Cherry Garden Pier at Rotherhithe; this is the place where vessels are supposed to sound a siren or let it otherwise be known if they want Tower Bridge opened for them. It is also one of the comparatively few places where maintenance men might conveniently meet a ship. *Grey Lash* waited for them there (and there we joined her). Some of the maintenance men arrived and were ferried out to her from the pier in a small boat (and some never appeared). Eventually *Grey Lash* set out on the next errand of the morning: to collect the empty barges *De Wit*, *Snow Thorne* and *Rodwell*, together with towing hand Jimmy Eves, from the South West India Dock.

Jimmy Eves, when sighted, seemed too smartly dressed to be a working lighterman, in well-polished shoes, neat trousers, and an anorak. In fact (though by inclination some men wear overalls) it is perfectly possible for a man to work with barges and remain as spruce as he likes. It is a lighterman's hands that need protection from the thick wet rope which constantly bears the strain of towing and being tied up, and becomes worn and frayed from all the chafing. So the men wear strong waterproof gloves.

At the South West India Dock the manoeuvres of tying and untying the barges were performed quickly and without fuss. There was no conspicuous throwing of ropes or leaping from boat to boat; the operation was carried out almost in silence and with the utmost care. Although few words were exchanged, a great deal of co-ordination is needed between tug captain and lightermen; the moving of the barges in the 'road' is aided by the tug's wash, and *Grey Lash* hovered around the proceedings with Dave Humphries watching alertly from the controls, every now and then revving his port or his starboard engine to provide a helpful wash which would propel a barge into place almost unaided by a lighterman. On a fine day the whole job looks deceptively simple and pleasant, and certainly physical labour is needed far less than in the past. Nevertheless bad weather can make the work almost as arduous and unpleasant as in the old days.

The barges collected from outside the South West India Dock were attached to *Grey Lash,* and the convoy then set off down river, while tea was brewed in the galley. The destination for *De Wit, Snow Thorne,* and *Rodwell* was Odams' Buoy at Silvertown, and the last of an ebb tide, still giving a perceptible advantage, saw the tug and barges rounding the great meander that forms three sides of the Isle of Dogs, and reaching their destination. Soon the three barges were being eased into position in the 'road', and their places astern of the tug were taken by *Rose Thorne* and *Olaf,* two more empty barges, to be taken down to Crayford Roads. The convoy set off again, passing Greenwich Gas Works and moving between the sign boards advertising the works on the new flood protection barrier. Soon *Grey Lash* was leading its barges past Woolwich Free Ferry, which carries foot passengers and vehicles between Woolwich itself and North Woolwich, Silvertown and the Royal Docks. Some of the last steam vessels on the Thames plied here, splendid paddle-steamers that were not replaced until 1963. Now the ferry is operated by two end-loading diesel boats, which constantly change place with apparent disregard for all other traffic, most disturbing to anyone inexperienced who proposes to cross their paths.

As at Deptford, shipbuilding at Woolwich was once the pride of the Tudor monarchs. But the Royal Dockyard closed in 1869, although mercantile shipbuilding and the famous Arsenal flourished here for a century more. A few vessels (such as offshore fishing boats) are built today at Woolwich, but the vast premises of Harland & Wolf lay empty and disused when we passed them. The site of the Arsenal, on the other hand, is at the beginning of a new life as Thamesmead, a river-oriented new town, while on the opposite bank the Royal Albert Dock is being reborn as the London Marina.

*Grey Lash* and her barges passed Thamesmead, on the right bank, and the Ford Motor Company's gigantic Dagenham works on the left. Passed too (also on the left bank) was another of the regular destinations of barges: Rainham Marshes, which are gradually being filled in with rubbish brought by water from the Grosvenor Canal and other points in Central London.

So we came to Crayford Roads, just beyond Erith, the most seaward point of this particular journey. Here *Grey Lash* left the empty barges, and turned round. At Erith Top Buoy *Trevose* was picked up, a single barge laden with some seventy tons of soya bean meal, a by-product of Unilever's soya oil plant at Erith. The tide had just turned, and the barges moored on swing-buoys were moving round to face in the opposite direction as *Trevose* was fastened on. Then tug and barge set off, up-river once more, to the British Oil & Cake Mills at Silvertown. These mills had, in fact, only a week left before their closure, and this was the last barge-load that Humphery & Grey would deliver to them. The destination was reached, *Trevose* was tied up, and soon, in the late afternoon, we were put ashore again at Cherry Garden Pier.

Closures are all too frequent along the tideway. Everywhere there are disused buildings, deserted wharves, dock gates that will never open again. But the tidal Thames has not yet given up its trade, and, like the other remaining lighterage companies, Humphery & Grey have continuing contracts which give them reasonable cause for optimism. Although the British Oil & Cake Mills have closed, and that particular 'run' has ended, the firm's barges still transport maize to the Millenium Mills for the processing of dog biscuits and other grain products, and to Wandsworth for gin. Meanwhile, the fashion of opinion in Britain is once again changing to favour water transport, perhaps just in time to save the barge-roads and the companies that do business in them.

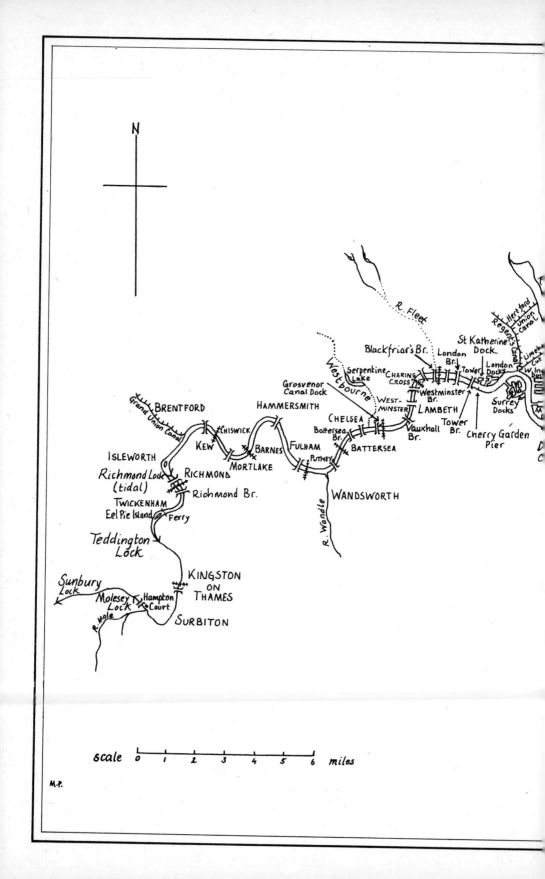

N

R. Fleet

Hertford
Union
Canal

Regent's Canal

St Katherine's
Dock

Westbourne

Blackfriar's Br.

London
Br.

Limehouse
Cut

W. Inc.

Serpentine
Lake

CHARING
CROSS

Tower

London
Dock

Grosvenor
Canal Dock

West-
MINSTER

Westminster
Br.

Surrey
Docks

Grand Union Canal

BRENTFORD

HAMMERSMITH

CHELSEA

LAMBETH

Tower
Br.

Cherry Garden
Pier

CHISWICK

Battersea
Br.

Vauxhall
Br.

ISLEWORTH

KEW

BARNES

FULHAM

BATTERSEA

Richmond Lock
(tidal)

RICHMOND

MORTLAKE

PUTNEY

TWICKENHAM

Richmond Br.

WANDSWORTH

Eel Pie Island

Ferry

R. Wandle

Teddington
Lock

KINGSTON
ON
THAMES

Sunbury
Lock

Molesey
Lock

Hampton
Court

SURBITON

R. Mole

scale   0   1   2   3   4   5   6   miles

M.P.

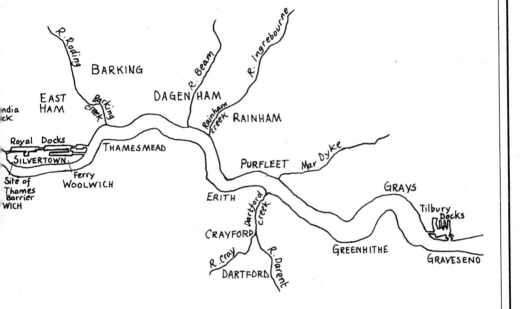

R. Roding
BARKING
EAST HAM
ndia ck
Barking Creek
DAGENHAM
R. Beam
R. Ingrebourne
Rainham Creek
RAINHAM
Royal Docks
SILVERTOWN.
THAMESMEAD
Site of Thames Barrier WICH
Ferry WOOLWICH
PURFLEET
Mar Dyke
ERITH
Dartford Creek
GRAYS
Tilbury Docks
CRAYFORD
R. Cray
R. Darent
DARTFORD
GREENHITHE
GRAVESEND

The Thames from Sunbury to Gravesend

# Index

# R

RAF Signals Command, 123
racing eights, 72, 73
Radcot, 42, 83
  Bridge, 42–5
  Weir, 35
  Lock, 103
Radley College, 76
Railway, Great Western, 24, 30, 77, 87, 101, 102, 111, 128
Rainham Marshes, 183
randan, 128
Ravensbourne, River, 175
Ray, John, 81
Reading, 66, 95, 103, 110
  Bridge, 107
regatta, 70, 121, 132
  Henley Royal, 69, 73, 113–21, 131, 133
Regent's Canal, 146
  Docks, 169
Regent's Park, 153
registration of boats, 30, 31, 103, 106
religious house, 33, 60, 64, 78, 84, 122, 123
Remenham, 121
Residential Boat Owners' Association, 150
Rhoden, Bill, 180
Richard I, 78
Richard II, 42
Richmond, 103, 164
Ridge's Weir, 37, 46
River Police, 173–5
Riverside Hotel, Burcot, 85
River Thames Society, 134
Romans, 2, 8, 27, 85, 158
Romney Lock, 100
Roper, William, 150
Rosamund's Well, 53
Rose, Bill, 74
  Sir Charles Day, 92, 94
  Tom, 72, 74
Rossetti, Dante Gabriel, 37–40, 41
Rotherhithe, 154, 169, 181
round house, 21, 22
rowing, 66–70, 73
  at Eton, 132
  eights, 67, 68, 72, 73, 104
  see also Doggett's Coat and Badge Race
  club, Oxford University, 67
  working men's, 89
rowing course, Henley, 118–9
  Oxford, 75
Royal Albert Dock, 169, 183
royal barge, 129, 135
Royal Dockyard, 175, 183
Royal Naval College (Greenwich), 176

Royal Swans, 127–8
Royal Swan Keeper, 126
Royal Victoria Dock, 169
Royal Waterman, 130, 131
Rugby, 91
Runneymede, 78, 134
Rushey Lock, 45, 99
Ruskin, John, 149
rymer and paddle, 33–7, 106

# S

Sadler, James, 113
sailing barge, 147, 165, 168–9
  see also Thames barge
St Bartholomew's Hospital (London), 156
St Edward's School (Oxford), 89
St John's Bridge (Lechlade), 26
St John's Lock (Lechlade), 2, 21, 99
St Katherine Dock, 164, 168, 169
St Patrick's Stream, 113
St Paul's Cathedral, 27, 156, 164
St Saviour's Dock, 153
Salter's Steamers, 65–6, 72, 86
Sandford Lasher, 75, 76
  Lock, 67, 75, 82, 102
  paper mill, 75
Sapperton Tunnel, 10–11, 23, 24
Sawyer, John, 5–7, 6
Seacourt Stream, 51
Second World War, 32, 77, 147
Serpentine Lake, 152
Severn, River, 26, 31
Severn Estuary, 9, 23
  ports, 3
  trows, 23
Seven Springs, 1, 2
sewage, 63, 103, 108, 109, 135, 156, 157, 164, 175
Shakespeare, William, 143
shallop, 142, 163
Shelley, Percy Bysshe, 31, 132
Shepperton, 135
  Lock, 101
Shifford, 45, 46
  Lock, 100, 103
  Lock Cut, 46
Shillingford Bridge, 85, 86
Shiplake, 113
  Lock, 98, 105, 113
  Weir, 113
Shrewsbury, Earl of, 124
Silvertown, 182, 184
skiff, 48, 66, 72, 73, 87, 120, 128, 132
Skinner, Joe, 37
Skinner's Weir, Bablock Hythe, 37